NEW ENGLAND LOCAL COLOR LITERATURE
A WOMEN'S TRADITION

Also by Josephine Donovan

Sarah Orne Jewett

Feminist Theory: The Intellectual Traditions
   of American Feminism

New England Local Color Literature

A Women's Tradition

Josephine Donovan

A Frederick Ungar Book

CONTINUUM • NEW YORK

1988

The Continuum Publishing Company
370 Lexington Avenue
New York, NY 10017

Printed in the United States of America

Library of Congress Cataloging in Publication Data

Donovan, Josephine, 1941–
  New England local color literature.

  Includes bibliographical references and index.
    1. American literature—New England—History and criticism.
  2. American literature—Women authors—History and criticism.   3. New
England in literature.   4. Local color in literature.   I. Title.
  PS243.D66 1982   810.9'9287   82-40252
  ISBN 0-8264-0415-4 (pbk.)

To
Henrietta Campbell Devigne
1877–1966
my grandmother

Contents

Acknowledgments

I would like to thank the following for their assistance to me in preparing various phases of this work: Barbara White, who generously shared with me her extensive knowledge of American women's writing; the Reference and Interlibrary Loan staffs of the University of New Hampshire, in particular, Jane Russell and Mel Regnell; Barbara Eckman, Marie Donohue, Judith Roman, Barbara Solomon, Philip Winsor, Margaret Hope, and Anne Barrett.

Introduction

On December 3, 1879, one hundred and four of Boston's—and the nation's—literary worthies gathered to mark the seventieth birthday of Oliver Wendell Holmes. The celebration was a birthday breakfast thrown by the *Atlantic Monthly*. In attendance were such notables as John Greenleaf Whittier, Ralph Waldo Emerson, Henry Wadsworth Longfellow, Samuel Clemens, William Dean Howells, Thomas Bailey Aldrich, T. W. Higginson, Charles Francis Adams, Jr., Henry O. Houghton, Horace Scudder, and James T. Fields. The publishers of the *Atlantic Monthly* had initiated the practice of celebrating the seventieth birthdays of their most distinguished contributors the year before, when Whittier reached his. In 1882 they continued the tradition for Harriet Beecher Stowe.

The Holmes event, however, was considered of particular significance because for the first time women writers were invited to an affair of this type. This was largely because the women had protested their exclusion from the Whittier breakfast, and the editors feared the rumored threat that the women planned to start a magazine of their own. Such a move—probably never seriously contemplated—would have been a real blow to the *Atlantic*, for from its first issue (November 1857) large numbers of its writers and readers had been women. A contemporary newspaper account of the Holmes breakfast called the invitation of the women "a new departure—a historical event, an innovation of a startling and a very important character."[1] The author of this report could not have understood its real significance, however, in the history of women's literature in the United States.

For it undoubtedly marked the first gathering of the New England school of women local colorists: Harriet Beecher Stowe (1811–1896), Rose Terry Cooke (1827–1892), Elizabeth Stuart Phelps (later Ward; 1844–1911), and Sarah Orne Jewett (1849–1909). Only missing was Mary E. Wilkins (later Freeman; 1852–1930), whose works had not yet begun to appear. Several other important literary women were also there: Annie Adams Fields (1834–1915), wife of publisher James T. Fields, both of whom played a central role in promoting the works of these women (see chapter 3); Julia Ward Howe, Helen Hunt Jackson,

Adeline Train Whitney, Abby Morton Diaz, Louise Chandler Moulton, Lucretia Peabody Hale, Rose Hawthorne Lathrop, and several others. Lydia Maria Child, one of the grandmothers of American women's literature, declined her invitation because of age.*

The newspaper account typically spent much time on the outfits worn by the women to prove that "literary work does not make women less handsome or less careful in dress, or less agreeable as wives, or less attentive as mothers." We learn that Rose Terry Cooke wore a "Worth dress" which "was, perhaps, a shock to one's sensibilities." But "to see Mrs. Stowe in an elegant black brocade with rare lace was pleasing; to behold Mrs. Julia Ward Howe in a Parisian costume of black and white silk" equally so. We learn finally that Rose Hawthorne Lathrop had a "perfect complexion and pearly teeth" and that Sarah Orne Jewett was "a tall and handsome brunette." Neither the habits of the men in attendance nor their looks are described.

The women themselves—Cooke, Stowe, Phelps, and Jewett—could not have realized the significance of their gathering, for they did not then (or later) think of themselves as a formal school. Yet they—together with Freeman—did eventually constitute a school whose contribution to American women's literature was considerable. They forged the tradition of realism that was bequeathed to such twentieth-century literary giants as Edith Wharton and Willa Cather, as well as Ellen Glasgow, Mary Austin, and later writers like Flannery O'Connor, Carson McCullers, and Eudora Welty.

The New England local colorists created a counter-tradition to the sentimental/domestic convention that dominated American women's writing through most of the nineteenth century. This book will show that when studied in historical sequence the works of Stowe, Cooke,

---

* I have had to make a decision whether to use the family or the married names of these writers. In the case of Harriet Beecher Stowe and Sarah Orne Jewett there was no problem. Each is so well known by her married and family name respectively—and each published nearly all her material under it—that there was no point in changing. Rose Terry Cooke, on the other hand, did publish much material under Rose Terry. However, after her marriage in 1873 she herself used Rose Terry Cooke, so I chose to follow her wishes. The same is true of Mary E. Wilkins Freeman, most of whose work was published under Mary E. Wilkins; however, she chose to use Freeman and so shall I. Elizabeth Stuart Phelps was the most difficult. She too married late and some of her late works were published under Elizabeth Stuart Phelps even after her marriage to Herbert Dickinson Ward, so I follow that choice, even though risking the possibility of confusion with her mother, who had the same name. The mother, however, wrote much earlier.

Phelps, Jewett, and Freeman illustrate the changing dimensions of a coherent, feminine literary tradition. The value and significance of their accomplishment has not received appropriate attention.[2]

The realism created by the local colorists must be seen in the context of the more general growth of realism in the Western tradition in the nineteenth century. But it must also be seen in the context of a centuries-old tradition of women's literary realism. This tradition, the contours of which are sketched in chapter 1, opposed itself to the sentimental romance, and promoted a critique of inauthentic female characters, in particular of what came to be called the "female quixote." Women's literary realism arose as a response to the real issues in women's lives—to their perceived lack of opportunities and to the role straitjackets against which women have railed for centuries. The tradition goes back at least as far as the fourteenth century.

Women's literary realism, as used in this study, could also be called "woman-identified realism." The term "woman-identified" was coined in the early years of the current women's movement to mean a woman who does not define herself in terms of a man personally, or in terms of institutions or ways of thinking that promote an ideology of male supremacy. Rather, her self-definition is generated from her identity as a woman, in alliance with other women, and through an assessment of her own realities, perspectives, and needs as a subjective consciousness, a human being.[3]

In literature by women one discovers, as early as the beginnings of the vernacular literatures, strains of realism that are "woman-identified." It is a realism which critiques "male-identified" or male-serving behavior, premises, and institutions, and which, on the contrary, promotes woman-identified ways of seeing and being. This woman-identified focus in literature I am calling "women's literary realism." It evolved out of the antiromance tendencies in the early novel, as noted in chapter 1, and was encouraged in its growth by the general movement toward realism in early-nineteenth-century literature.

The New England local colorists, however, presented the first women's literary tradition which moved beyond a negative critique of reified male-identified customs and attitudes. The New England women created a counter world of their own, a rural realm that existed on the margins of patriarchal society, a world that nourished strong, free women. The culmination of this tradition is to be found in Jewett's master-work *The Country of the Pointed Firs*.

The significance of this woman–identified vision lies in the fact that it represents the first sustained literary representation of women that is not based on the sentimentalist "heroine's text" (discussed in chapters 1 and 2). This male–identified text, which dominated literature about women for over a century, repeated a fundamental plot where the heroine must deal with the pressures of a male seducer. Nancy K. Miller, who coined the term, notes that there were generally two variants: either the woman succumbed and was therefore punished; or she held out and was rewarded, usually with a proper husband. It was "crucially dependent upon the uses and abuses of [the heroine's] chastity."[4] As Miller points out, this issue really dominated fiction by and about women throughout the eighteenth and well into the nineteenth century. Hardy's *Tess of the D'Urbervilles* is a latter-day example, but scores of American sentimentalist works followed the "heroine's text" or variants thereof. The New England local colorists, however, derived from an alternative tradition and created a world-view of their own that had little or nothing to do with this kind of "heroinism."

The local color school's production of authentic works of women's literary realism did not last into the twentieth century. By the 1880s one detects in the literature a growing note of anxiety and disillusionment. The prolonged struggle for women's rights, which seemed to go on endlessly through the nineteenth century and with little discernible progress (women still did not have the vote by the turn of the century, even though the Anthony Amendment had been introduced in Congress in 1878), may have contributed to a growing sense of frustration and disillusionment among women writers. Reflective of such pessimism was Charlotte Perkins Gilman's "The Yellow Wallpaper," a Kafkaesque description of women's oppression which appeared in 1892. By then a sense of defeat is evident in the works of Elizabeth Stuart Phelps; of elegy in Sarah Orne Jewett, and of bitter disillusionment in Mary E. Wilkins Freeman—a theme carried on by Edith Wharton in the early years of the twentieth century.[5]

Historian Nancy Sahli suggested that a cultural shift in society's attitude toward women and in women's attitudes toward themselves began to occur in the last quarter of the nineteenth century. She identified the shift as a "fall" that became manifest around 1875.[6] It involved the dissolution and consequent derogation of the close female networks that had obtained during the earlier Victorian era.

This study tends to corroborate the Sahli thesis. Proceeding inductively from the works themselves I have noted that they seem to reflect and to express a transition away from a reverence for female activities, values and traditions toward one that favored and promoted androcentric cultural institutions. I have organized my study around this idea.

In general, the early works describe and promote a society in which women are (or, it is assumed, should be) in the ascendency. This remains the dominant vein in local color literature. However, the later works reflect the intrusion of an ideology of male supremacy. Of course, the transition is not "neat" in chronological terms; yet it is clear. By the turn of the century female bonding had given way (for the most part) to heterosexual marriage, usually with women in subordinate roles. Rural women's traditions of knowledge—herbology, witchcraft and ecological holism—were threatened by male institutions of scientific-industrial knowledge. Mechanization, rapid transportation and communication systems were promising to recolonize forever the matriarchal worlds of the New England local colorists.

Thanks to pioneer works of feminist literary criticism like Elaine Showalter's *A Literature of Their Own* (Princeton: Princeton University Press, 1977) it has become evident that women writers do have traditions of their own that are separate from men's. This does not mean that all women writers partake of a women's tradition, as Ellen Moers pointed out,[7] but that there are some women writers who more comfortably belong grouped with one another. The New England local color school is one such group.

The attempt to define a literary school and to specify the mechanics of influence is a notoriously difficult critical enterprise. The term "school" implies a teacher–student relationship between a master and a group of usually younger disciples.[8] In this case, while neither enunciated a coherent set of aesthetic principles, Harriet Beecher Stowe and, to a lesser extent, Rose Terry Cooke functioned as the group's leaders by creating the models of the form that the "disciples" would use. There is no question, therefore, of the *influence* Stowe and Cooke had on their followers. This influence will be demonstrated throughout this study. Suffice it to note here that all these women knew and corresponded with one another and read one another's works with great appreciation.

The school's original theoretical underpinnings, or justifications, were laid down by the early editors of the *Atlantic Monthly*: namely James Russell Lowell, who edited the magazine from 1857 to 1861; James T. Fields, 1861–71; William Dean Howells, 1871–81; Thomas Bailey Aldrich, 1881–90; and Horace Scudder, 1890–98. These men through theoretical statements (mainly Lowell and Howells), editorial selections, and personal encouragement of the women authors deserve credit for the early growth of the movement. T. W. Higginson should also be added to the list, for several of his theoretical articles were of considerable importance. These included "A Letter to a Young Contributor" (1862), "Literature as an Art" (1867), "Americanism in Literature" (1870), all in the *Atlantic*. Young Mary E. Wilkins, for example, heard Higginson lecture in 1870. Undoubtedly his words had an effect.[9]

These men can be—and have been—criticized for promoting a realism that was too genteel (especially Fields, Aldrich, and Howells). It is a criticism that has some validity. In her autobiography Elizabeth Stuart Phelps relates how when she read *The Story of Avis* (1877) aloud to the Fieldses prior to publication, he was offended by a scene where a man stays up late at the piano with a woman friend while his wife is upstairs in bed. Fields cried, ". . . no, no! Not that! . . . Keep the story above that!" As Phelps points out, the most that happened in the scene was that the two held hands.[10] Nevertheless the *Atlantic* was the first magazine to reject blatant sentimentalism, and as Frank Luther Mott noted, under Lowell it became "a great force" for the production of "more realistic, vital fiction."[11]

Lowell's realist aesthetics were enunciated in the first volume of the magazine in a review of George Eliot's first major work, *Scenes from Clerical Life* (1857). Lowell took the occasion to excoriate "romance writers," who fail "to copy Nature faithfully and heartily"—an expression of the realist doctrine of mimesis: "Sometimes . . . a daring romance-writer ventures . . . to represent a heroine without beauty and without wealth. . . . But after a time his resolution fails;—each new chapter gives a new charm to the ordinary face; the eyes grow 'liquid' and 'lustrous,' [and the character] is transformed . . . into a commonplace, tiresome *novelesque* Beauty."[12] Lowell praises Eliot's work, however, for its unpretentiousness and for its veracity of detail: "The greater part of each story reads like a reminiscence of real life, and the personages introduced show little sign of being 'rubbed down' or 'touched up and varnished' for effect." Fred Lewis Pattee suggests that this sentence "explains the position of Lowell: he demanded real life and not dreamings about life."

He was attracted by the genuineness and truth to life in a tale, be it high life or low, and he rejected without hesitation the mechanically literary, the artificially romantic, and the merely sentimental. With the advent of *The Atlantic Monthly* a healthy realism for the first time decisively entered American fiction.[13]

William Dean Howells also rejected sentimentalism for its fraudulence, and favored works that bordered on nonfiction. As Everett Carter notes, ". . . he encouraged writers to give him stories about people and places they knew, without worrying about plot or incident." Further: "When books came across his reviewing desk which contained truthful characterizations in clearly observed settings, he cheered for them . . . when the pieces he received were lacking in these elements, he would ask the contributor to get more sense of 'locality' into his [her] stories and articles."[14]

The term "local color" is traditionally used to apply to a literary movement that was in some sense transitional between romanticism and realism, but the theoretical statements of the *Atlantic* editors make it clear that the intentions from the beginning were toward realism. The first genuinely local color stories were those which depicted authentic regional detail, including authentic dialect, authentic local characters, real geographical settings, authentic local customs and dress. While the term was first used in the *Atlantic Monthly* in 1864 (to apply to George Eliot's *Romola*),[15] the tradition really reaches back at least as far as an eighteenth-century Irishwoman, Maria Edgeworth (see chapter 1).

The tradition necessarily favored women writers, for like the domestic novel, it allowed them to describe their own bailiwicks, realms that they knew intimately. It did not require heroic experiences on an epic scale that they themselves could never have had. It allowed them to express their own concerns on a scale reflective of their own experience. The moral vision that emerges in the works of these New England women is very much rooted in their awareness and concern about woman's situation in the nineteenth century—which was after all their condition.

Two philosophical issues endemic to American local color literature—the rural–urban dialectic and the transition from a belief in salvation by grace to salvation by works (and perhaps back again, in Freeman)—are transformed in these women writers' handling into issues that express female moral dilemmas.

Bernard R. Bowron, Jr., presents an excellent theoretical discussion of the evolution of local color literature and its growth toward realism in a 1951 article, "Realism in America."[16] Bowron suggests that local color literature was the "agrarian wing" of American realism, because of its "generally nostalgic mood and its exploitation of preindustrial [non-urban] milieux" (273). Implicit in many local color works was a critique of urban industrialism. The New England women local colorists were not, however, pastoral romantics. Indeed, one of the most intriguing devices they used—that of the outsider-narrator—suggests a certain ambivalence toward rural life, seen especially in the later writers.

The women writers' concern and interest with preindustrial life stemmed from their situation as women. Rural life in nineteenth-century New England had become predominantly matriarchal or female-centered. Many young men had been killed in the Civil War, or had left to seek their fortunes in the West or in urban centers. This meant that the world left behind was, so to speak, a world controlled by the mothers and their values. The New England local colorists depicted this matriarchal world positively and lauded its nourishment of strong women characters and their traditions of women's culture, such as herbology and witchcraft. The imaginative vision construed from this world provided an important counterweight to industrial capitalism and to Calvinism, which are implicitly (and sometimes explicitly) perceived by these writers as male systems.

Bowron notes that local color writers often expressed what became a creed among the realists: an optimistic belief in salvation by works. Setting the literature in the context of American theological dialectics, Bowron argues that it carried forth the views of human salvation advanced by the Arminian heresy (much earlier known as the Pelagian heresy)—that of a doctrine of individual free will and of redemption through the choice of committing good works, which, following the Second Great Awakening (1797–1831), implied a commitment to moral reform.[17] Significantly, two of the authors in this study, Elizabeth

Stuart Phelps and Harriet Beecher Stowe, were born into families whose patriarchs had been closely associated with the Second Great Awakening: Moses Stuart, Phelps's maternal grandfather, and Lyman Beecher, Stowe's father. Phelps's paternal grandfather, her father, Austin Phelps, and Stowe's husband, Calvin Stowe, were all ministers. Needless to say, Phelps and Stowe were steeped in theological doctrine, as are their works.

The Arminian position was, of course, a radical departure from the Calvinist doctrine of salvation by grace. One may see in the early works of the New England local colorists a movement away from the arbitrary and irrational concept of the Calvinists, which is perceived as a masculine tyranny, and toward a more liberal, rational, and humane notion of regeneration. This transition is, to be sure, not restricted to these women writers. The "feminization" of American religion was a general cultural drift that occurred in the society at large during the century.[18] But a humanized religion that emphasized accessible salvation through individual works was an essential part of the matriarchal vision of Stowe, Cooke, Phelps, and even Jewett.

Harriet Beecher Stowe, herself a much stronger feminist than is generally recognized, began her literary career with a strong repudiation of the sentimental romance, which she saw as a European product, and which she rejected in favor of authentic, realistic depiction of her own American environment—one which she saw as nourishing authentic and strong women. Like the other local colorists Stowe followed the realist doctrine of mimesis; she nevertheless shaped the givens of her rural world into a reflection of her own female concerns and desires.

While the doctrine of mimesis implies that art consists of an exact transcription of reality, it must be pointed out that no writers are such automatons that they transcribe reality completely objectively with no organization, no selection, no evaluation of their material. Such indeed would not be art. Sarah Orne Jewett became aware of the contradictions implicit in the notion of mimetic realism, which she knew she was going far beyond, and coined the term "imaginative realism," which came close to symbolism, to explain what she was doing (see chapter 7).

It is becoming a central tenet of feminist literary criticism that the controlling vision which guides most if not all women writers in shaping their material reflects their interests and concerns as women. And so it is with the writers of the New England local color school. Stowe turned New England into a kind of female Arcadia. Rose Terry Cooke registered a disenchantment with rural life, however, and was the first to depict the grim realities of the lives of rural women, especially wives, isolated on farms. But she also continued in other of her works Stowe's vision of a countryside that promotes women and their culture. With Phelps, Jewett, and Freeman one senses, however, a growing note of discordance—of uneasiness and ambivalence—a sense of having to deal with the demise of this female Utopia, a sense that this matriarchal world is falling apart.

One final question need be addressed in this introduction: Why restrict the list to these five? Why not also Alice Brown, Helen Hunt Jackson, Harriet Prescott Spofford, Agnes Trumbull Slosson, Rebecca Harding Davis, Mary Murfree, Kate Chopin, Constance Fenimore Woolson, Grace King, etc.? I chose these five because they form a recognizable school and because each illustrates significant moments in the evolution of this women's literary tradition. Each was a major writer who produced an impressive volume of literature over a sustained period of time. With the possible exception of Phelps all were great writers. Stowe, Cooke, Jewett, and Freeman produced works that are most certainly masterpieces, by any standard of critical judgment. Their relative obscurity is undeserved. One result I would hope from this study would be a redirection of attention to these writers and a renewed appreciation of their contribution to Western literature.

1

Toward the Local Colorists: A Theoretical Sketch of Their Sources

In order to properly understand the place of the New England school of women local colorists in the continuing traditions of women's literary realism, it is necessary to go back to the origins of modern, vernacular literature, to the origins in particular of the novel. The novel took shape as a bourgeois genre and promoted from the beginning an antisentimental, antiromance, realistic vision. One of the earliest examples of the novel, *Don Quixote*, is indeed constructed as a burlesque of the heroic romance.

Women's literary realism grew out of the bourgeois critique of the romance, but it expressed an awareness and concern about female characters and female roles which the male writers' critiques did not, for it was rooted in female self-interest. This critical awareness is evident in the earliest novels by women in the eighteenth century, and even before, in critical statements made as early as the fourteenth century by Christine de Pisan. Women's realism is drawn in opposition to falsely sentimental, inauthentic female characters (seen in the romance), and to artificial and unjust restrictions placed upon the female role by society.

The antiromance sentiment of the early male novel is transformed into a satire of the "female-quixote" figure in the women's tradition, and the early male novelists' obsession with female seduction becomes transformed in certain women's novels of manners into a satirical critique of the marriage market. A culmination of both tendencies is to be found in Jane Austen's novels. The "female quixote" is satirized in the figure of Catherine Morland in *Northanger Abbey*, while the marriage market rituals receive ironic treatment in *Pride and Prejudice*, and, to a lesser extent, *Sense and Sensibility*.

The novels of manners provide a negative critique of social mores that are inimical to women, and therefore express a kind of feminist realism. But the traditions we are tracing did not derive chiefly from Austen and the novel of manners. For, the local colorists' great accomplishment, indeed, was that they did not remain negatively fixed upon the destructive practices of patriarchal society; rather they created a positive, other world of their own that promoted powerful and independent women.

It was Maria Edgeworth, not Jane Austen, who originated this tradition. In Edgeworth's works are found not only the central motifs of women's realism seen in the novel of manners, such as the "female quixote" and the marriage market satire. More important, she created a provincial world that stands counter to the establishment world of urban patriarchy. Such a rural world was to become central to the vision of the American local colorists. Edgeworth's importance in women's literary history lies in her identification with the provincial outsider—the Sancho Panza of *Don Quixote*—against the dominant class. The ironic antiromance perspective provided by a provincial, peasant-class male in *Don Quixote* becomes in Edgeworth's novels the perspective of women's critical realism. This chapter will trace these developments from *Don Quixote* to Maria Edgeworth's *Castle Rackrent* and *The Absentee*.

Ancient critical authority held to a doctrine that literature be ranked in importance according to the social milieu it depicted. The highest form, tragedy, was that which dealt with royalty. Domestic life, urban street life, rural or peasant life were only appropriate subject matter for comedy, which was considered a lower form of literature. Bourgeois women and their domestic world were not considered appropriate subjects for serious literary treatment.

Most literature in succeeding centuries followed the ancient assumption that important literature deal with the upper classes, and usually with males. During the late Middle Ages a new form, the courtly love romance, became popular in aristocratic circles. The romance presented highly idealized women characters, almost always of the courtly class. Courtship and passion were the central subjects of these works. This aristocratic genre, the romance, continued on well into the seventeenth century, succumbing finally, due to a variety of historical circumstances, to a bourgeois genre, the novel.

The novel developed, in part at least, as a critique of the heroic romance. *Don Quixote*, the most important of the early novels, was constructed upon a burlesque of *Amadís de Gaula*, a popular heroic romance. At the same time the novel incorporated some of the values and assumptions of the romance, and thus from its beginnings presented a conflict between two worlds: one that of the aristocracy and the other that of the bourgeoisie, or as Erich Auerbach put it, between the "idyllic and the everyday." In *Don Quixote*, Auerbach notes, "the two realms of life and style clash."[1] Since the governing perspective in the novel is that of bourgeois or common-sense realism, the aristocratic vision is depicted as foolish and unrealistic. The collision is that between what Jane Austen later labeled "sense" and "sensibility." The device used to negate the world of sensibility is that of comic irony; Sancho continually debunks Don Quixote.

As a bourgeois form the novel necessarily dealt with economic realities, a subject never raised in ancient tragedy or in the aristocratic romance. Novels dealing with bourgeois women, which began to appear in increasing numbers in the early eighteenth century, necessarily saw them in terms of their economic status. Bourgeois women were propertyless and financially dependent; unless they were under the aegis of a father or a guardian, they were in dire circumstances. The fundamental plot pattern that developed in this bourgeois or sentimental novel dealt centrally with women's economic plight. It remained unchanged for over a century.

From Marivaux's *La Vie de Marianne* (1731–41), the prototype of the sentimental novel (preceding even *Pamela*), to Susan Warner's *The Wide, Wide World* (1851), an American sentimentalist best-seller, the essential pattern remained the same: an orphaned girl, who is disinherited and abused by a variety of suitors and/or guardians, finally recovers her father and her patrimony and/or marries, thus establishing her economic security, which is to say, thus achieving happiness, in this bourgeois vision.

At their worst these novels dwelt upon the despoliation of the innocent orphan, who moves about as in a jungle, beset at every turn by a seducer-rapist. In this "heroine's text" the woman can either reject the harassment and proceed to the happy ending, or if she is in fact raped, as in Richardson's *Clarissa Harlowe*, and her innocence—and therefore her market value—destroyed, she must die.[2] Thus the courtship motif of the romance is in the male bourgeois handling turned into a seduction/victimization pattern, rooted, however, in economic reality.

The sentimentalist bourgeois novel sometimes criticized the romances directly by having the heroine read, or reject the reading of, romances, seeing them as delusions that mislead young women into thinking that they will be saved by miraculous white knights who speak in courteous platitudes. Such delusions make them game for seducers when they should be protecting their virtue and reputation in order eventually to establish their economic security. *Pamela's* subtitle, *Virtue Rewarded*, implies this ethic. In this sense *Pamela* and most of the novels of this type may be seen as reworkings of the Cinderella or Griselda myth.[3] The latter, a popular late-medieval figure, proved her worthiness by remaining faithful to her husband despite severe trials.

Henrietta (1758) by Charlotte Lennox is a novel that shows most graphically the two-tiered nature of the bourgeois sentimental novel. In this work Lennox satirizes an upper-class woman who is lost in precious romance fantasies, while the main plot concerns the trials and tribulations of the disinherited bourgeois orphan on her quest to reclaim her economic status.

When Henrietta first meets Miss Woodby in a stagecoach, the gentlewoman immediately perceives their relationship in terms of the literary romance. They must, she suggests, call each other Clelia and Celinda and consider that they have contracted "a violent friendship." Henrietta responds, "Call me what you please . . . but my name is Courtenay." Miss Woodby hopes aloud that her new friend does not have an "odious vulgar Christian name; such as Molly or Betty or the like."[4] Later they discuss shepherds and shepherdesses, stock articles in the pastoral romance. Henrietta acknowledges that when she was fourteen she had hoped to see one "in a fine green habit, all bedizened with ribbons . . ." (1:72). The reality, however, was that she found "the shepherd was an old man in a ragged waistcoat . . . the shepherdess looked like a witch . . ." (1:73). Here we have an obvious debunking of romance fantasy from the point of view of common-sense or bourgeois realism. Lennox's extended satire of the heroic romance and its effect on gullible young women is to be found in *The Female Quixote* (1752) discussed below.

Henrietta represents the world of sense, as opposed to Miss Woodby's sensibility. The latter trait proves to be so impractical as to be treacherous, and Henrietta learns that hardheaded perseverance is the primary means to survival. In the course of her trials Henrietta is reduced to working as a servant, clearly perceived as a fate worse than death in this bourgeois world (*Pamela* reflects this class bias, as do most novels of the eighteenth century). Nevertheless, Henrietta has chosen a servant's life in preference to others even more disagreeable—being married to an evil rake or being confined in a convent—and therefore her voluntary servitude gives evidence of her basic integrity, as well as her fortitude. Her spirit of independence is seen in her proud comment ". . . since I have learned not to fear poverty, my happiness will never depend upon others" (2:123). And in her rejection of a disagreeable suitor: ". . . if you had worlds to bestow on me, I would not be your wife" (2:158). We find, therefore, even in certain sentimental novels, which rework the so-called "heroine's text," an intrinsic critique of the romance and the beginnings of realism in the depiction of women characters.

Like *Henrietta*, Samuel Richardson's *Pamela* (1740–41) reflects the breakdown of *Stiltrennung*, or the classical separation of styles, as Ian Watt has pointed out in his history of the novel.[5] The clash between classes is resolved when Pamela Andrews, of a lower class, marries Lord Davers, an aristocrat. The difficulties of this cross-class liaison are fully addressed at the end of the first volume: she could no longer socialize with the servants, but the women of his class would not socialize with her; this is resolved by her determining to learn various domestic occupations so that she will not miss social involvement.

Perhaps the first sense of women's critical realism in the Western tradition may be seen in the writings of Christine de Pisan (c. 1364–1430), who was among other things the first feminist critic. In her epistles on the *Romance of the Rose* (*L'Epistre sur le Roman de la Rose*, 1400, and in particular *L'Epistre au dieu d'amours*, 1399) Pisan protested against misogynistic and stereotypical treatment of women in the late medieval romance.

In *L'Epistre au dieu d'amours* Pisan says that she has received complaints from all manner of women over the defamations, deceptions, and ridicule they regularly endure from men. The women also complain of misogyny in literature, in particular in Jean de Meun's *Roman de la Rose*, which expends countless pains and efforts to deceive one innocent maiden. "Does such a feeble target," Pisan asks, "require so great an assault?"[6] "I respond to them," she continues, "that the books were not written by women" (line 409). "If women had composed the books, I know for sure that the facts would be otherwise, for they well know that they have been wrongly enculpated . . ." (lines 417–19).

Not too long after (in 1589) an Englishwoman, Jane Anger (probably a pseudonym), similarly protested the literary mistreatment of women, in particular that seen in John Lily's *Euphues his Censure to Philautus*, another romance. Without knowing about women and because they lack such imaginative understanding, Anger wrote, men "fall straight to dispraising and slandering" our sex.[7]

Mary Delariviere Manley (1672–1724), one of the earliest women novelists, wrote an excellent critique of the romances in her preface to *The Secret History of Queen Zarah* (1705). Perhaps the first woman after Pisan and Anger to question the authenticity of most female characters in the romance, she said the women characters "did not act as women act in life."[8]

Manley's own roman à clef, *The Adventures of Rivella* (1714), one of the earliest examples of the genre in English, expresses a worldly, Machiavellian cynicism and a feminist realism that is a far cry from the sentimental romance. The cynicism, fairly typical in seventeenth-century letters, is reminiscent of that seen in La Rochefoucauld or in Ben Johnson's *Volpone*. The world is portrayed as a decidedly unromantic jungle in which people operate primarily according to self-interest. Romantic idealism is often seen to be a façade masking cynical motives.

Manley allegedly wrote this work as a kind of personal defense against false public slander. It is supposed to be mainly autobiographical. The novel opens with a clear statement of feminist realism:

Her vertues are her own, her Vices occasion'd by her Misfortunes; and yet as I have often heard her say, *If she had been a Man, she had been without Fault*: But the Charter of that Sex being much more confin'd than ours, what is not a Crime in Men is scandalous and unpardonable in Woman, as she herself has very well observ'd in divers Places, throughout her own Writings.[9]

With this indictment of the double standard Manley asserts that she is concerned with the truth. "She loves *Truth*, and has too often given her self the Liberty to *speak*, as well as write it" (14).

The narrator of *Rivella* is an ex-suitor, Sir Charles Lovemore. He acknowledges he loved her in his youth, ". . . but she did not return my Passion, yet without any affected Coyness, or personating a Heroine of the many Romances she daily read" (18). Here we have an early critique of the stereotypical romantic heroine, as distinguished from the realistic protagonist, Rivella.

Rivella's basic philosophy of self-interest is announced: "Rivella was always inclin'd to assist the Wretched; neither did she believe it Prudence to neglect her own Interest, when she found it meritorious to persue it . . ." (65). She goes through a number of unfortunate experiences, each time growing more disillusioned, finally retiring into seclusion to write. "She told me her Love of Solitude was improved by her Disgust of the World . . ." (41). The work is sprinkled with tart perceptions of others. Of one friend Manley notes, "Calista who was the most of a *Prude* in her outward Professions, and the least of it in her inward Practice . . ." (66). (Since the figures in the work were thinly disguised versions of real individuals, it is not surprising that the work was considered scandalous.)

Another early work which reflects a nonromantic feminist realism is Jane Barker's *A Patch-Work Screen for the Ladies* (1723). This curious proto-novel purports to be constructed in the fashion of a patchwork quilt. The plot is a seemingly autobiographical narration of the trials of a young girl, interspersed with comments in the tradition of women's critical realism.

Galesia has had ambitions to be a writer and yet realizes such is not considered appropriate for a woman. But though she acknowledges that her "Fingers ought to have been imploy'd rather at the Needle and the Distaff, than to the Pen and Standish," she nevertheless tries her hand at various forms of poetry.[10] She attempts to educate herself by reading works of science (this in part an attempt to forget a failed love affair). But she soon realizes that a "Learned Woman [is] . . . like a Forc'd-Plant, that never has its due or proper relish" (11).

After her father dies she is suited by a "train of Pretenders." But she refuses to "act the Coquet" or to affect the "formal Prude," both stereotypical behavior patterns of the romantic heroine. She then moves to London with her mother, where Barker presents a satirical critique of foppish city ladies; Galesia cannot adapt to their ways ("the Curtesies, the Whispers, the Grimaces, the Pocket Glasses, Ogling, Sighing, Flearing, Glancing . . .") (46). An implicit contrast is drawn between the rural world of Galesia's birth and the phony world of urban society—a contrast that will take on much greater significance with Maria Edgeworth and the local colorists. "The *Assemblèes* [sic], *Ombre*, and *Basset-Tables* were all *Greek* to me, and I believe my Country Dialect, to them, was as unintelligible" (43).

Galesia decides to retire from this "Beau World" in order to study in solitude. During this time she turns her studies to good effect and achieves modest fame as a local physician. This may well be the first example of the professional woman in literature. "People came to me for Advice in divers sorts of Maladies, and having tolerable good Luck, I began to be pretty much known" (55). She acknowledges that "Pride and Vanity" were "to some Degree united to this Beneficence; for I was got to such a Pitch of helping the Sick, that I wrote my *Bills* in *Latin*, with the same manner of *Cyphers* and *Directions* as Doctors do; which Bills and Recipes the Apothecaries fil'd amongst those of the Doctors" (56). In her excitement over her success as a doctor she writes a poem of self-praise: ". . . *I celebrated my own Praise . . . for want of good Neighbors to do it for me . . .*" (59). Galesia's mother encourages her to marry but she remains attracted by the "Single Life" (90).

We have in Galesia an authentic female character, self-motivated, with an active critical consciousness, who is far removed from the vapid heroines of the romance. Throughout this novel are found vignettes describing the oppressed lives of many of her compatriots and realistic glimpses of daily life of the time. At one point Galesia even complains of London's air pollution, saying, "Air, abstracted from Smoke, is not to be had within Five Miles of *London*" (67). This in 1723!

Sarah Fielding's *The Adventures of David Simple* (1744) also includes strong, realistic portraits of women. One of these is Cynthia, a natural feminist who has a critical perception of women's lot. As a child, she says,

"I loved reading, and had a great desire of attaining knowledge; but whenever I asked questions of any kind whatsoever, I was always told, such things are not proper for girls of my age to know. If I was pleased with any book above the most silly story or romance, it was taken from me—for miss must not enquire too far into things, it would turn her brain; she had better mind her needlework, and such things as were useful for women! reading and poring on books would never get me a husband."[11]

She especially resents the fact that her brother "hated reading to such a degree, that he had a perfect aversion to the very sight of a book; and he must be cajoled or whipped into learning, while it was denied me, who had the utmost eagerness for it" (111). She had a close female friend who also loved reading, but Cynthia's mother forbade them to spend too much time together. "My mother was frightened out of her wits, to think what would become of us, if we were much together. I verily believe, she thought we should draw circles, and turn conjurers" (117).

David Simple presents one of the first extended critiques of the marriage market rituals. The feminist assertions of the heroine are notable. When Cynthia's father decides she should be married, she remarks sarcastically that she hopes she will get to see her husband-to-be "at least an hour beforehand" (117). When the selected future husband informs her that he and her father had agreed on the match, she retorts, "I did not know my father . . . had any goods to dispose of . . ." (119). The suitor reveals a traditional concept of wifedom: she must keep house, etc. She responds that she had "no ambition to be his upper servant" (120) and calls such an arrangement "prostitution." She also rejects the use of the wife as a status symbol, using the analogy of "the horse who wears gaudy trappings only to gratify his master's vanity" (120).

Cynthia is punished for her rebelliousness. Her father disinherits her, and after he dies she must make her own way in the world. After various misfortunes she inherits money and marries the brother (Valentine) of her old friend Camilla, whom David, the protagonist of the novel, marries.

Eliza Haywood's *The History of Miss Betsy Thoughtless* (1752) carries forward the critique of the marriage racket, seeing it as a cat-and-mouse game: "The young lady was full of meditations on her new conquest, and the manner in which she should receive the victim."[12] This novel also contains one of the first critiques of marriage itself. Betsy's first marriage is unhappy: "Is this the state of wedlock?" she wonders, "call it rather an Egyptian bondage" (4:47). In one particularly painful moment her husband kills her pet squirrel, anticipating by nearly two centuries Susan Glaspell's celebrated story "A Jury of Her Peers" (1917). Fortunately for Betsy, however, her husband finally dies, so she is free to wed again; this time the match is happier.

The History of Jemmy and Jenny Jessamy (1753), also by Haywood, though sentimental in mood, presents another female protagonist who is thoughtful, actively in control of her life, and who resists the mindless courtship rituals advanced by the romances. An earlier work by Haywood, *Anti-Pamela* (1741), is a straightforward social satire of the gold-digging husband hunter. It also provides a strong critique of the romantic heroine, suggesting that her antics are simply ruses to capture her intended victim, a husband. Syrena Tricksy

had not reached her thirteenth year, before she excell'd the most experienced Actresses on the stage, in a lively assuming all the different Passions. . . . Agitations adapted to the Occasion, her Colour would come and go, her Eyes sparkle . . . she would fall into Faintings . . . and all this so natural, that had the whole College of Physicians been present, they could not have imagin'd it otherwise than real.[13]

While Haywood could perhaps be accused of blaming the victim in this novel, her critique nevertheless implies an awareness of the hypocrisy forced upon women by economic realities. Thus it is not too far from Haywood and the other early women realists to Mary Wollstonecraft's *Vindication of the Rights of Women* (1792), the first sustained feminist treatise. Wollstonecraft too decried the ridiculous manners expected of women and urged that equal education would strengthen women's critical faculties to see the underlying economic and political reasons for their behavior.

The ultimate expression of the antiromance tradition in English women's literature was Charlotte Lennox's *The Female Quixote* (1752). This novel satirized the seventeenth-century romances by Mlle. de Scudéry and La Calprenède in much the same way that Cervantes had ridiculed *Amadís de Gaula* in *Don Quixote*.

The heroine, Arabella, steeped in the romances she has been reading, comes to see the world in their terms. She expects all men to behave as the heroes of romances, to contract "violent passion" for her, to write her secret gallant letters, to carve her initials on trees, etc. Of course, all who hear of her notions think her mad. One amusing example is an assistant gardener, taken by Arabella to be a "Person of Quality" who has dressed up as a gardener in order to be near her. "She often wondered . . . that she did not find her Name carved on the trees . . . that he was never discovered lying along the Side of one of the little Rivulets, increasing the Stream with his Tears."[14]

Lennox's novel is especially important because its influence may be traced in a direct line to the American women's literary tradition. Its successor is Tabitha Tenney's *Female Quixotism* (1801), a popular American novel. Another probably more important influence Lennox had was on Maria Edgeworth—Edgeworth herself perhaps the most important influence on American women writers of the first half of the nineteenth century.[15] Especially significant and obvious was her influence on Harriet Beecher Stowe. Early American women critics from Lydia Maria Child to Margaret Fuller praised Maria Edgeworth for promoting positive down-to-earth models of womanhood.[16]

Sandra Gilbert and Susan Gubar have suggested that Edgeworth's masterpiece, *Castle Rackrent* (1800), be read as "a subversive critique of patriarchy."[17] Indeed, the images of women presented in the novel do reveal a feminist awareness. One woman is locked up by her husband for seven years. More significant, however, is her satirical treatment of Miss Isabella, a pretentious sentimentalist, who becomes the wife of Sir Conolly Rackrent. The narrator of the novel is Thady Quirk, "an illiterate old steward" of the Rackrent family, who speaks in a "vernacular idiom."[18] Thus, the novel is about the masters—the Rackrents, the aristocrats—told from the point of view of middle-class realism. Once again we see the basic dialectic of the novel as it was in its origins: a critique of aristocratic pretensions. Now, however, the critique of the patriarchs is from a feminist point of view.

Miss Isabella is a classic example of the romantic, aristocratic, male-identified heroine. The narrator considers her to be a "mad woman" (43), because she threatens to faint at every step, wears a veil, uses precious sentimental language, reads romances (*The Sorrows of Werther*, in this case). In short, she is a reincarnation of the female quixote.

The use of local dialect by the narrator, as opposed to the Rackrents, who speak correct English, is one of the first examples of dialect use in English literature. Dialect became popularized by Sir Walter Scott in the Waverley novels, but Scott acknowledged his debt to Edgeworth in his General Preface to the collected novels. Of course dialect use became the hallmark of the local color tradition in America, with the same curious class associations drawn between it and standard English. We shall explore this further in subsequent chapters.

Edgeworth also followed the antiromance female quixote tradition in her moral tale "Angelina; or l'Amie Inconnue." Here again the heroine inbibes romances to the point where she functions in their terms.

Once again the common-sense world is peopled by provincials who speak in dialect and do not act like heroes in romances. The climax is the meeting between Angelina and Araminta, a woman she had known only through gallant correspondence. Araminta turns out to be a "coarse, masculine, brandy-loving creature, engaged to an equally coarse, vulgar man, Nat Gazebo," whose epistolary name had been Orlando.[19] An aunt rescues Angelina from her folly and has her read *The Female Quixote* as penance.

Edgeworth's importance in the continuing traditions of women's literary realism that led to the American local colorists can be seen most clearly in *The Absentee* (1812). In this novel the upper-class establishment world of London society is satirized from the point of view of the Irish outsider, who affirms in the end the validity of her provincial world.[20] The Irish homeland is perceived as a kind of Utopia—anticipating the Utopian New England village of the local colorists—where women can behave as honest, normal human beings, not as society gold-diggers or romantic fops.

The novel revolves around the figure of Lady Clonbrony, who has convinced her family to live in England, leaving their Irish homeland (hence operating as "absentees") and denying their Irish heritage. Lady Clonbrony affects an English *haut monde* accent that fools no one. One observer notes facetiously, ". . . you *cawnt* conceive the *peens* she *teekes* to talk of the *teebles* and *cheers . . .* and with so much *teeste* to speak pure English."[21] Lady Clonbrony is struggling between two selves: one is her natural, "real," Irish self; the other, her pretentious, novelesque, English self. In this sense she is another version of the female quixote. "A natural and unnatural manner seemed struggling in all her gestures . . . —a naturally free, familiar, good-natured, precipitate, Irish manner, had been schooled, and schooled late in life, into a sober, cold, still, stiff deportment, which she mistook for English" (6). She slips back into an Irish accent when she is talking about her adopted niece's attachment to her. The relationship with the niece, Grace Nugent, is presented as unaffected and genuine; Grace is held up in the novel as a model of unaffected authenticity.

Lady Clonbrony's son, Lord Colombre, is the victim of various husband-hunting mothers, and indeed his own parents seek to marry him to an heiress since their financial situation is tenuous. The son, however, finally convinces the family to return to their proper environment, Ireland, and he marries the "real" heroine of the novel, Grace

Nugent. What convinces Lady Clonbrony to return to Ireland is the knowledge brought back by her son that an Irish tenant, the Widow O'Neil, had remembered her fondly over the years. The affectional tie with ordinary provincial people proves decisive.

Edgeworth is therefore one of the first authentically local color writers: she authentically portrays realistic Irish characters, customs, and dialect in a realistic historical setting. Moreover, her political and emotional tie is to this provincial world. It is solid, honest, unpretentious; set in opposition to the false, hypocritical world of the upper-class, in this case English, establishment. For the first time we have the suggestion that women's freedom from the social oppression of the urban marriage market rituals lies in a return to the local world of the provinces. This is very different from Jane Austen's novel of manners where the rituals are simply transposed to a provincial (but still upper middle-class) setting. None of Austen's central characters are authentically regional; they do not speak in dialect. It is Edgeworth, therefore, who carries forward the traditions of women's literary realism and articulates the world-view that is inherited most directly by the American school.

Before crossing the ocean and picking up the American traditions one further English figure need be noted: Mary Russell Mitford. Mitford's significance is not nearly so great as Edgeworth's, because she presents little or no moral vision in her work. Nevertheless, her masterpiece, *Our Village* (1824–32), was extremely influential as a form of fiction which later women writers found congenial.

Our Village is a series of sketches of local life in a provincial English town. The narrator is a woman, an insider who lives in the town and knows everybody's history. The format of some sketches is that the narrator takes a walk with her dog, a greyhound named Mayflower. (Harriet Beecher Stowe's first published collection, *The Mayflower*, may conceivably be a veiled tribute to her predecessor in the genre of the village sketch, though of course it refers mainly to the Pilgrims' ship.) On her walks with Mayflower the narrator encounters someone, often a village eccentric, who triggers an anecdote, or she describes the landscape, the particularities of various houses, and seasonal variations in vegetation. The general mood is one of affectionate humor. There is an implicit assertion that this world is a model realm, but there is little or no articulated rejection of urban, patriarchal civilization.

Mitford pioneered the village sketch tradition, which continued as the dominant form used by the American local colorists as well as by Englishwoman Elizabeth Gaskell in *Cranford* (1853). One could also perhaps see George Eliot's earliest work, *Scenes from Clerical Life*, as emerging from this tradition, though Eliot's moral vision is so strong as to effectively change the form into something quite different.[22] We will now see how the village sketch fared in the American context, and how, infused with Edgeworth's moral world-view, it became the vehicle of American women's realism in the hands of the New England school of local colorists.

2

Toward the Local Colorists: Early American Women's Traditions

Three novels which are representative of early and divergent traditions in American women's literature are Susanna Rowson's *Charlotte, A Tale of Truth* (first published in this country in 1794, and better known as *Charlotte Temple*); Tabitha Tenney's *Female Quixotism: Exhibited in the Romantic Opinions and Extravagent Adventures of Dorcasina Sheldon* (1801); and Catharine Sedgwick's *A New-England Tale; Or, Sketches of New-England Character and Manners* (1822).

Charlotte Temple is an archetypal example of what Nancy K. Miller has labeled the "dysphoric heroine's text." It recounts the seduction and abandonment of a young innocent, who eventually gives illegitimate birth and dies in disgrace. Charlotte is the quintessential victim: she is physically delicate, incapable of any kind of self-motivated decision, and completely unsuspecting and defenseless before even the most basic of the world's realities. When, for example, near the end of this rather lengthy novel, Charlotte, having been abandoned with child, discovers that she must pay rent money, she is completely bewildered. "She never had bestowed a thought on the payment of the rent of the house. . . ."[1] Her solution to this dilemma is to set out on foot for New York City in the dead of winter in summer clothes. Needless to say, she is not long for this world, and dies soon after.

The author, perceiving that there is little that is redemptive about this woeful tale, issues an aside to the reader in which she urges a Christian moral, that of the purifying value of suffering (148). One has a sense that Rowson tacked this moral on ex post facto so to speak, for the seduction story she repeats in *Charlotte Temple* is really a Richardsonian male script that perceives woman as victim and appears to have been written at least in part for the titillation of male readers. I do not question Rowson's sincerity, however; she apparently gleaned the details of the story from real life and believed herself to be writing a cautionary tale. It was not long, nevertheless, before women critics—Lydia Maria Child and Margaret Fuller, for example—were enjoining young female readers against reading this kind of story. Child singled out *Charlotte Temple* as "especially vicious" in *The Mother's Book* (1831).[2]

Nevertheless, it is important to note that Rowson's ostensible moral view is that Charlotte has earned a kind of moral or spiritual triumph by dint of her sufferings. That is, because she has endured extreme pain with no thought of rebellion, she appears to be a natural candidate for sainthood. This fundamentally Christian notion repeats the Cinderella or Griselda model for female behavior, which we have seen is typical of this kind of novel. While Charlotte was not rewarded with a handsome prince, she did achieve redemption, while all the evil characters in the novel, including Charlotte's seducer, are punished. (The fact that their punishment comes at the very end and that the bulk of the work focuses on Charlotte's troubles suggests strongly, however, that this is a male-directed script.)

Far different but also fundamentally unoriginal in conception is Tabitha Tenney's *Female Quixotism*, which is a reworking of the by-then well-established female quixote plot. The story is set in the United States, however, and includes some realistic details of setting and character that distinguish it from its predecessors. Tenney was also a highly inventive comic genius; many of her episodes are quite original and extremely amusing. This is one of those lost novels that bears retrieval. It appears that, unlike Charlotte Lennox, who used the French romances as her satiric target, Tenney returned to the original *Don Quixote* for her source. The comic flavor is similar.

Tenney issues an antiromance statement at the beginning of the novel:

Now I suppose it will be expected that, in imitation of sister novel writers . . . I should describe her as distinguished by the alabaster skin, heavenly languishing eyes, silken eyelashes . . . aquiline nose, ruby lips . . . and azure veins, with which almost all our heroines of romance are indiscriminately decorated. In truth she possessed few of those beauties. . . . Her complexion was rather dark; her skin somewhat rough; and features remarkable neither for beauty nor deformity.[3]

Dorcasina's counterpart is her servant Betty, who presents the viewpoint of common-sense realism, continually debunking her mistress's romantic visions. Betty speaks in a mild dialect, using incorrect grammar. There is also a black servant Scipio, who speaks in dialect.

The antipretentious humor in certain episodes anticipates the vein of humor characteristic in local color works where also we find urban, upper-class, male-identified pretensions debunked. At one point an elderly Dorcasina, who by now looks like a scarecrow but retained illusions of romantic beauty, keeps losing her wig (2:181). The episode comes very close in spirit to Sarah Orne Jewett's "The Dulham Ladies" (1886), where two elderly sisters don faddish "frisettes" in a vain attempt to appear attractive. Interestingly enough, Jewett and Tenney appear to have been blood relatives. Both were connected to the Gilman family of Exeter, New Hampshire.

Tenney, therefore, brought the antiromance across the ocean, where it continued to flourish in the works of the local colorists. That the perspective of comic irony is in this novel associated primarily with a rural working-class woman is also a significant form repeated in local color fiction, although in Tenney's handling it does not accede to the level of significance of Maria Edgeworth's use of provincial figures. There is inherent in Tenney's work, as perhaps in any comic vision, an underlying sense of rational optimism; that is, the assumption is that if people see clearly and shed themselves of illusory thinking, they can arrange their lives soberly and rationally. In this sense, too, Tenney initiates an American tradition that leads directly to the local colorists.

Catharine Sedgwick's *A New-England Tale* is often cited as a benchmark work. Nina Baym establishes it as the first of the genre of "woman's fiction" that so dominated American women's literature in the nineteenth century, labeled the sentimentalist/domestic tradition by others.[4] Sedgwick dedicated her work to Maria Edgeworth because of the latter's commitment to morally instructive fiction. Indeed, Sedgwick has been called the American Edgeworth, a sobriquet that is to my mind highly misleading. For it is primarily only the moralistic aspect of Edgeworth's work that Sedgwick reproduced, although in *A New-England Tale* there are touches of the novel of manners with its inherent critique of marriage-marketing in the figure of Mrs. Wilson, who "indulged [her daughter's] passion for dress, in hope that the glittering of the bait would attract the prey."[5] But there is little of Edgeworth's wit or sense of comic irony and little or no sense of local realism (despite the title). There is one eccentric character, a witch-figure, Crazy Bet, who prophesies and sees through town sham, but she is not integral to the plot.

The plot is the archetypal "euphoric heroine's text"[6] that underlies most if not all sentimentalist fiction: Jane Elton is essentially orphaned early in the novel and farmed out to a nasty relative, Mrs. Wilson, who, as noted, spends her time promoting her daughter's marriage opportunities and being mean to Jane. In this variant of the Cinderella text Jane finally moves out to accept a teaching position, and is rewarded in the end with a benign and worthy husband.

There is no question that Jane Elton is a step forward from Charlotte Temple. She is assertive; she speaks back forcefully on occasion; she has her own ideas; she makes decisions. Indeed, a substory enclosed within the novel concerns an orphaned woman who had been seduced and abandoned with child. Jane confronts the seducer, and while she does not really defeat him, nevertheless does not herself succumb to the evil schemers in the novel.

A New-England Tale reflects, on one level, a transition away from the notion of salvation by grace toward the idea of salvation by works. It is symptomatic of the theological and cultural shift that is beginning to occur in the country at the time, a transition that will also be seen in the local colorists' works. And it also expresses a certain entrepreneurial optimism that active engagement in public work will earn success: the Horatio Alger myth. This becomes an important component in sentimentalist fiction, seen perhaps most dramatically in Hannah Lee's *Elinor Fulton* (1837), where the pragmatic heroine works day and night to support her family and in the end is rewarded not just with economic success but also with a husband. As in many of these novels *Elinor Fulton* ironically includes a diatribe against the women's rights movement, and argues for "the supremacy of the other sex."[7]

A New-England Tale, Elinor Fulton, and others of the genre remained trapped within a preestablished Cinderella (or Griselda) script, for the underlying pattern in these works—no matter how assertive the heroine may appear—is that of the trials and tribulations of a morally pure innocent whose suffering, patience, and endurance are in the end rewarded with Mr. Right. (Or, who, in the rare cases where the heroine does not marry, achieves a moral and spiritual triumph. This usually, however, requires her death, as in Mrs. E. D. E. N. Southworth's *Retribution* (1849), and is therefore more "dysphoric" than "euphoric.")

Susan Warner's *The Wide, Wide World* (1851)—an inadvertently ironical title, for the world of the novel is narrow, domestic, and invested with female solipsism—is fairly characteristic of the genre. It was indeed one of the most popular of the sentimentalist works. In this novel Ellen Montgomery is soon orphaned and farmed out to an unsympathetic aunt. At first Ellen has an impertinent Shirley Temple-type streak of talking back and asserting herself, but she learns eventually to control herself and behave in a properly submissive Christian way. After years of trials of one kind and another Ellen is rewarded with marriage. Though the novel is set in at least one exotic locale—Scotland—there is little or no sense of local detail and no sense of historical context. The plot is engaged entirely with Ellen's fortunes and misfortunes and in this sense is characteristically solipsistic. The rhetoric ranges from the hyperbolic emotionalism characteristic of the genre to a generally polite formal discourse. There is no naturalism in dialogue or dialect (except for an extremely minor character in Scotland who speaks in brogue). There is little or no humor, no sense of comic irony, and little or no subtlety in character development or motivation.

Another example may be cited to round out this discussion of the genre so as to establish clearly the character of the dominant women's tradition of the century, the backdrop against which the local colorists forged their own tradition. Augusta Jane Evans's *St. Elmo* (1866), in many ways one of the most interesting of the genre, concerns Edna Earl, another orphan brought up by strangers. The opening description of Edna gives a good example of the form's characteristic rhetorical extravagance and shows how close the sentimentalist vision remains to that of the romance: "The young face, lifted toward the cloudless east, might have served as a model for a pictured Syriac priestess. . . . The large black eyes held a singular fascination in their mild sparkling depths, now full of tender loving light and childish gladness; and the flexible red lips curled in lines of orthodox Greek perfection."[8] This is precisely the kind of romantic description that Tabitha Tenney and her antiromance predecessors debunked over and over, and which the countertradition of local color realists will continue to critique.

Like many of the sentimentalist heroines, Edna is interested in self-improvement (in the American myth receiving an education is one of those obstacles that, once endured, is believed to yield instant success, and for sentimentalist women success meant love and marriage). Edna makes it clear that she has no desire to become a "blue stocking" or to use her education in any productive way. She indeed excoriates the women's rights movement as the "most loathsome of political leprosies" (393). Finally her endurance and moral purity are rewarded: the man she has loved, St. Elmo, who has had all the earmarks of an evil rake early in the novel (he had even killed a man in a duel), becomes a minister and therefore an acceptable marriage partner. And so they marry.

By contrast, the local colorists eventually reject this broadly defined Cinderella script. In the works of Jewett and Freeman in particular the heroine as often as not rejects the seducer-suitor (when that is even an issue) and chooses a life of her own. And marriage or the arrival of Mr. Right is hardly set up as a redemptive justification for suffering. On the contrary, beginning with Rose Terry Cooke the local colorists began to examine the realities of married life—something the sentimentalists rarely did—and they found these hardly bore comparison to the romantic myth.

Sarah Orne Jewett's "A White Heron" (1886) may be seen as the culmination of the repudiation of the Cinderella text carried forth by the local colorists. In that justly celebrated story a young girl, who has been brought up in a rural environment and who knows the birds and animals of the woods intimately, is called upon by a potential suitor to reveal to him the whereabouts of a rare white heron that he wishes to kill and stuff for his collection. She hesitates but after much agonizing remains loyal to her female woodland sanctuary, refuses to reveal the bird's location, and therefore essentially rejects the seducer-suitor figure, the "handsome prince." Significantly, in the Grimm version of the legend Cinderella's dead mother had returned in the form of a white bird. The further implications of this story will be discussed in chapter 5; suffice it to note here that it signals the end of the Cinderella text: in Jewett's story the heroine takes her life in her own hands, rejects the prince, and remains loyal to her matriarchal environment.

Tendencies towards realism appear in American women's writing before the local colorists in a minor tradition that existed side by side with the much more visible and popular sentimentalist tradition. Sarah

Josepha Hale was one of the most powerful promoters of the sentimentalist "cult of true womanhood," which preached piety, purity, submissiveness, and domesticity as primary female virtues.[9] She is remembered primarily for her role as editor of the influential sentimentalist *Godey's Lady's Book*, which, nevertheless, published some of Harriet Beecher Stowe's earliest local color stories in the 1840s. Hale also, however, published fiction of her own—some of which had realistic tendencies.

Her novel *Northwood* (1827), though essentially a romance, was perhaps the first work to include real details of the New England locale. Lydia Maria Child's *Hobomok* (1824), which antedates *Northwood* and which purports to have a realistic setting, is really a historical romance with little or no realism, though it is still a readable novel. *Northwood* was also probably the first novel to paint rural New England as a kind of Utopia. Later, more memorable examples include Elizabeth Stuart Phelps's *The Gates Ajar* (1868), Stowe's *Oldtown Folks* (1869), and Jewett's *The Country of the Pointed Firs* (1896).

Hale's novel begins with a significant apologia that is a variant of the antiromance manifesto that by then was becoming a commonplace. "Mine," she asserts, "is a relation of domestic events, a description of simple manners and retired scenes. I have no titled personages to show off, no warrier [sic] with stern brow and nodding plume to threaten or combat."[10] She claims she wishes to be known not for "imitation of popular authors" but for the "delineation of scenes faithful to nature" (1:4).

Hale does include scenes of local description. Northwood is pinpointed geographically in Rockingham County on the turnpike between Concord and Portsmouth, New Hampshire, all real places. Local vegetation and landmarks are described realistically, and a lengthy Thanksgiving dinner is recounted in minute detail, though there is little sense of historical context. The women characters are stereotypical; they are quiet, obedient, never offer opinions, and spend their time on domestic chores. A central female character is described as "the brightest angel of domestic bliss" (1:209), and a wedding is described in the rapturous tones of pure romance. There is also a critique of the selfish belle-figure, a topos that derived from the Edgeworthian novel of manners and that continued as a commonplace in the early local colorists; particularly was this a hobbyhorse of Harriet Beecher Stowe.

Hale also published *Sketches of American Character* in 1829. This work was perhaps the first in the American "sketches" tradition that derived from Mary Russell Mitford's *Our Village* (though Sedgwick's *New-England Tale* was subtitled *Sketches of New-England Character and Manners.*)[11] Mitford herself published in *Godey's* as early as 1833. Hale's sketches appeared in the 1820s in *The American Ladies' Magazine and Literary Gazette*, which she edited before it merged with *Godey's* in 1837.

These short pieces do express a definite sense of local New England detail. Some of the characters have localized names, such as Ezekiel Clark. There is a certain antiromance sentiment. Clark's daughter is named Fanny. "That was her name; had she ever attended a boarding school it would probably have been *novelized* into Frances; but the advantages of a fashionable education she never had enjoyed, and so I shall call her . . . Fanny."[12] Here one may note the early identification of the romance with urban education and before long with European civilization—all of which is seen as pernicious in contradistinction to the real, simple, authentic lives and manners of indigenous Americans. Hale, and Stowe after her, as true Jacksonians, were chauvinistically American and concerned to delineate and affirm authentically American rural mores.

Nevertheless, the plots of Hale's sketches are essentially sentimental romances, although in "The Village Schoolmistress" and "William Forbes" are found the first of a long line of New England spinsters portrayed relatively positively, if conceived primarily in terms of failed romance. Hale also carries on the Edgeworthian critique of *beau monde* watering places, in this case Saratoga Springs, New York, in a sketch entitled "The Springs"; she puts down the belle type in "The Belle and the Bleu"; and she includes one of the first temperance stories in "The Wedding and the Funeral."

Catharine Sedgwick also produced a number of short stories or sketches during the late 1820s and 1830s, collected as *Tales and Sketches* in 1835. None of these are of great interest, except for the fact that they are generally anchored in real settings. One story, however, "Mary Dyre," published originally in *The Token for 1831*, a gift annual, is modeled on an historically true story about a Quaker woman martyred on the Boston Common.

Sedgwick's preface to the story is a realist manifesto:

The subject of the following sketch, a Quaker martyr, may appear to the fair holiday readers of souvenirs, a very unfit personage to be introduced into the romantic and glorious company of lords and ladye loves; of doomed brides; and all-achieving heroines; chivalric soldiers; suffering outlaws; and Ossianic sons of the forest. . . . Neither have we selected the most romantic heroine that might have been found. . . . We have passed over these tempting themes to tell a briefer story, and present a character in its true and natural light, as it stands on the historic page, without the graces of fiction, or any of these aids, by which the romance writer composes his picture—exaggerating beauties, placing them in bright lights, and omitting or gracefully shading defects.[13]

Unfortunately, while the story itself may be a real one, the narration devolves into melodramatic emotionalism and therefore it belongs more in the sentimentalist than in the realist camp. This tendency toward romantic hyperbole when describing horrible historical or social realities continued to plague women writers through the nineteenth century. Rebecca Harding Davis and Elizabeth Stuart Phelps were prone to this weakening indulgence.

The village sketches tradition continued in a little-known work by a little-known but talented writer, Charlotte A. Fillebrown Jerauld, whose *Chronicles and Sketches of Hazlehurst* appeared posthumously in 1850. The first of these is believed to have been written as early as 1843.

Jerauld is the first American woman writer who planted herself firmly on the side of rural life, as Maria Edgeworth had, and who saw it threatened by encroaching industrialism manifested by the arrival of the railroad. Like Hale she mistrusts urban education, which she foresees as destructive of rural customs: "Alas . . . the follies and fashions of the great world have stolen in upon us, and are making fearful devastation upon the minds and manners of the people."[14] She laments how young girls go off to fashionable boarding schools, returning "with mincing gait and affected lisp . . . to ridicule what to their fastidious ears is the unintelligible, vulgar jargon of their parents . . ." (364). Like others before and after, she perceives village life as Utopian but sees it as a world that is passing—due largely to the effect of the railroad. "In the good old days, before the railroad came within half a dozen miles of Hazlehurst . . ." she begins (370). "Forthwith, on the banks of our beautiful streams, arose saw-mills and grist-mills, manufactories of cotton and combs, machine-shops . . ." (371). This anti-industrial sentiment became a hallmark of women's literary realism from Rebecca Harding Davis and Elizabeth Stuart Phelps to Jewett and Freeman.

Jerauld describes authentic details of her rural New England environment in a fashion similar to Mitford, and employs the device of the insider narrator-persona who takes the reader along "our village" paths as a kind of tour guide. "On the right of the main or stage road . . . is a cross-path which was always a favorite walk of mine . . ." (416). The narrator proceeds to identify the inhabitants of each house in a style that borders on nonfictional matter-of-factness. Unfortunately, the stories themselves are largely cast in the romance format. The narrative technique, however, became a standard organizing device in local color fiction. But in Jerauld, unlike later local colorists, there is little uncertainty about the narrator's identity. She belongs *in* the village, though she has enough knowledge of the outside world to be defending her native soil against urban "progress."

The culmination of this early tradition of village sketches was Harriet Beecher Stowe's *The Mayflower; Or, Sketches of Scenes and Characters Among the Descendents of the Pilgrims*. This collection, which appeared in 1843 but included stories published as early as 1834, was really the first work in the tradition of local color realism and as such will be treated in chapter 4.

The village sketch tradition continued in weakened but still popular form in Emily Chubbuck [Judson]'s *Alderbrook: A Collection of Fanny Forrester's Village Sketches, Poems, Etc.* (1846). The lead story in this collection, "Grace Linden," is another anti-industrial piece that anticipates Davis and Phelps in its depiction of "the dark, dirty factory, with its strange machinery . . . its greasy blackened walls and disagreeable smells."[15] Such touches of realism are marred by a sentimentalist heroine who eventually marries and lives happily ever after, the evils of factory life forgotten. Two other pieces extol rural life, "Underhill Cottage" and "Little Molly White," but essentially the work is that of sentimentalist moralism. Alice Cary's *Clovernook or Recollections of Our Neighborhood in the West* (1851) continued the tradition, but it lacked a precise descriptive sense of local detail and tended toward sentimentalism in character and plot.

Perhaps the most important of the early women writers who contributed to the growth of local color realism was Caroline Kirkland.

Though Kirkland focused primarily on life in the then Western states—
and therefore does not fall within the parameters of this study—her influence was considerable. Edward Wagenknecht in his study of Harriet
Beecher Stowe notes that the young Stowe was familiar with Kirkland.
And, in a hitherto unnoted 1856 letter, Rose Terry Cooke also revealed
a positive acquaintance with Kirkland's work.[16]

Kirkland believed herself to be writing in the tradition of Mary
Russell Mitford. In her preface to *A New Home—Who'll Follow?* (1839)
she notes that it is obvious "that Miss Mitford's charming sketches of
village life must have suggested the form of my rude attempt."[17] Later
she says she wishes Mitford had written these tales (9), referring to
them as "crayon-sketches of life and manners in the remoter parts of
Michigan" (v).

Kirkland claims to faithfully record events and characters as she saw
them with little or no embellishment. Her work is "an unvarnished
transcript of real characters, and an impartial record of every-day
forms of speech . . ." (8). She calls it further "a meandering recital of
common-place occurrences—mere gossip about everyday people, little
enhanced in value by any fancy or ingenuity of the writer" (19). Kirkland's self-deprecating apologia is not merely the pose of modesty typical of the woman writer of the period; it also heralds the realist's ideal
of faithful mimesis with little or no authorial interference.

Kirkland, however, does not fail to comment on events. Indeed,
many of them seem shaped to make a moral or political point. In this
she differs markedly from Mitford. Like others of the American
women realists she is strongly opposed to capitalist exploitation—one
of her most celebrated passages in *A New Home* condemns the "tricksy
spirit" in frontier land speculation (53–55). She also opposes alcoholic
indulgence; several episodes have a pro-temperance moral.

Significantly, she associated the capitalist mentality with men. "Men
look upon each one, newly arrived, merely as an additional business-
automaton—a somebody more with whom to try the race of enter-
prize, i.e. money-making," whereas women had "a feeling of hostess-
ship toward the new comer" (109). In one temperance sketch Kirkland
reveals a profound sympathy with female oppression. The master of
the inn is in a drunken fury. His "wife and children were in constant
fear of their lives. . . . I can never forget the countenance of that desolate woman, sitting trembling with white compressed lips . . ." (14).

Kirkland was also motivated by a strong antiromance sentiment. Annoyed by the false romantic fantasies of the West promoted in works like Chateaubriand's romantic idyl *Atala* (1801), Kirkland hoped to set the record straight, to show what life was *really* like on the frontier.

The circumstance of living all summer, in the same apartment with a cooking fire, I had never happened to see alluded to in any of the elegant sketches of western life which had fallen under my notice. . . . I had . . . dwelt with delight on Chateaubriand's Atala where no such vulgar inconvenience is once hinted at; and my floating visions of a home in the woods were full of important omissions, and always in a Floridian clime, where fruits served for *vivers* (83).

Kirkland's work includes real details of the environment, and her characters are authentic local figures who speak in dialect. Two strong women characters explode the "cult of true womanhood" and are real literary foremothers of the great female characters created by the local colorists: (Stowe's) Grandmother Badger in *Oldtown Folks* and (Jewett's) Mrs. Todd in *The Country of the Pointed Firs*. Mrs. Danforth, a hostess at a frontier inn, is the first of these. She kills rattlesnakes without batting an eye and says she'd "as lief meet forty on 'em as not" (30). The other is the village "schoolma'am," Cleory Jenkins, who smokes tobacco in a pipe—"(not 'Pan's reedy pipe,' reader)" (95).

Kirkland also ridicules the "female quixote" figure who seems particularly absurd in the frontier context. In one episode, a Miss Eloise Fidler, imbued with romantic novels, longs for a lover with a French name, and wears impractically elegant clothes in the wilds. She never removes her gloves, and her shoes are so fancy she cannot go outdoors. "This piece of exquisite feminine foppery [meant] eternal imprisonment within doors, except in the warmest and driest weather . . . indeed somewhat of a price to pay . . ." (174). Of another starry-eyed couple she suggests that rather than bringing *Atala* or *Gertrude of Wyoming* to the frontier, it would have been more practical to have brought *Buchan's Domestic Medicine, The Frugal Housewife,* and *The Almanac* (269–70). Kirkland, therefore, carried the village sketch tradition far beyond its genteel origins and paved the way for the growth of a genuine women's realism.

Another minor current which contributed to the emergence of local color realism was a tradition of native humor. Much of this humor was written by men and thereby reflected a male perspective; one common anecdote involved wife-beating.[18] The first published woman humorist was Frances M. Whitcher. Her *Widow Bedott Papers* was originally published in the 1840s in *Neal's Saturday Gazette* and in *Godey's*, but was collected for posthumous publication in 1855 by Alice Neal [Haven].

The Widow Bedott Papers, which was very popular (the first edition sold 100,000 copies and it went through five editions), is essentially about a rural rustic's attempts to snare a husband. The widow is herself the narrator. Indeed the narrative is a kind of breathless monologue in which the widow speaks to an unheard interlocutor whose response is never given. The widow talks in a rural, misspelled dialect, and part of the humor lies in her roundabout never-get-to-the-point style, which is interspersed with homey comments like "Pass the bread." The widow's humor is from a feminine point of view; her favorite book is about a woman who killed five husbands.

Alice B. Neal, who edited the Whitcher work posthumously, wrote on her own a series of comic sketches entitled *The Gossips of Rivertown* (1850). This work is a satire of town gossips and the harm they do but it veers toward moralism, and therefore loses the comic punch of the *Bedott Papers*.

The local color realists drew from these antecedents but forged of the materials an essentially new tradition, the first in American women's literature that authentically reflected American women's issues. Before proceeding to an analysis of their works, it seems appropriate to examine the literary and social context in which their school developed.

3

Annie Adams Fields and Her Network of Influence

Literary creation does not happen in a desert. Or, if it does, it blooms unseen. To have an audience—that is, to fully exist—literature depends upon a production network. Very few writers create a substantial body of work without being connected to such a network. Women have historically been cursed by lack of access to such male-controlled media. The New England women writers were favored, however, by having such access, and by having a woman friend as a central publishing power. Their local color school could not have existed without the Boston publishing network that surrounded and issued from James T. (1817–1881) and Annie Adams Fields (1834–1915).

James was one of the founders of and eventually senior partner in the Boston publishing house of Ticknor and Fields. This firm, one of the most powerful of the time, eventually became Fields, Osgood and Co. and finally Houghton Mifflin. In 1859 Ticknor and Fields purchased the young *Atlantic Monthly*, and from 1861 to 1871 Fields was the magazine's editor.

His wife, Annie Adams (they married in 1854), fully participated in his publishing activities, and became a writer of minor repute in her own right. Her most substantial contribution was, however, editorial—both in the editorial decisions she made on his behalf in selecting materials for publication and in the several "life and letters" books she put out in later years. These latter included *Life and Letters of Harriet Beecher Stowe* (1897) and *Letters of Sarah Orne Jewett* (1911). Hardly models of scholarship (they are heavily edited), they nevertheless provide important period materials for researchers.

Both James and Annie were strong supporters of women writers and both became advocates of women's suffrage. James was early enamored of Mary Russell Mitford, met her in England, and included selections from a lengthy correspondence with her in his reminiscences *Yesterdays with Authors*. James's judgments were not, however, always infallible. He reportedly told Louisa May Alcott, for example, that she has "no talent for writing."[1] Nevertheless, the Fieldses supported Louisa's literary efforts both materially and morally. In 1862 they let her use a room in their house, and they gave her $45 a month toward her rent. Louisa was a cousin of Annie's through the May family.

But this was not simply a matter of family ties. Annie made the Fieldses' townhouse at 148 Charles Street a veritable hospice for aspiring, as well as established, authors. Young Rebecca Blaine Harding (later Davis), another budding talent the Fieldses personally tended, has recorded the heartening effect they had upon her.

Rebecca, a native of Wheeling, West Virginia, had made a spectacular debut in the *Atlantic Monthly* with her powerful "Life in the Iron Mills," which appeared in the April 1861 issue. Her next contribution, "A Story of To-Day," which later became the novel *Margaret Howth*, continued her depiction of wretched factory working conditions. Fields found the story too grim and asked her to revise it. But he also asked Annie to write her encouragement, which she did. Fields published "A Story of To-Day" in the October issue of the *Atlantic*.

The Fieldses urged Rebecca to visit them in Boston, which she did in the spring of 1862. Rebecca later noted how Annie's greeting had dispelled her feelings of being "scared and lonesome" in the bustling city, and thus began what became "Rebecca's closest and most supporting literary friendship."[2] The intensity of that bond is recorded in a letter Rebecca wrote to Annie shortly after her marriage to Clarke Davis: "My dear *dear* Annie: I wanted to write before only to say I love you . . ." (118). Davis went on to have a significant effect on Elizabeth Stuart Phelps (see chapter 5).

Rebecca was neither the first nor the last woman to form an intense friendship with Annie Fields. Indeed, Annie became the emotional center of an extended circle of women writers, including those of the local color school. For several, including Harriet Beecher Stowe, poet Celia Thaxter, and Sarah Orne Jewett, Fields was probably the most important adult relationship they had.

Stowe's biographer, Forrest Wilson, records how Harriet Beecher Stowe first met the Fieldses at a reception in Florence, Italy, in 1860. "In such a romantic setting . . . Harriet met her future publisher and the woman who was to be her most intimate friend during the remaining years of her life." "Annie Fields," he further notes, "not yet twenty-six that Florentine evening, was a brilliant woman, already a shining figure in the Boston literary firmament and soon to be something of a dictator in it; but in the sudden presence of the little Andover authoress she became a trembling schoolgirl, abashed and uncertain of herself."[3] Stowe by this time was already a near-legend, having published *Uncle Tom's Cabin* in 1852. The Fieldses and the Stowes returned together to the United States in 1860 on the steamship *Europa*. Also on board were the Nathaniel Hawthornes. Hawthorne's major works, too, had been published by Fields, starting in 1850 with *The Scarlet Letter*.

Harriet's lifelong correspondence with the Fieldses began after this voyage. Like many another woman writer Harriet often addressed the letters jointly or wrote directly to Annie in order to reach James. As Wilson notes, ". . . when she wanted to carry a point with the *Atlantic*, Harriet addressed this letter to [them] jointly, no doubt expecting the adoring Annie to act as her friend at court" (464).

An 1864 letter to James from Stowe illustrates the role Annie played. The letter refers to an article she was working on which urged the reader to "buy American" during the Civil War. "Dear Friend Fields . . . Please let Annie look it over & if she & you think I have said too much of the Waltham watches make it right. . . . If Annie thinks of any other thing that ought to be mentioned & will put it in for me she will serve both the cause and me."[4] Another example of Annie's influence may be seen in a letter to her from Julia Ward Howe. Howe had sent some poems to James a week previously and had not heard from him. The letter to Annie prods, "Please tell Mr. Fields that I am waiting to hear from him about the poems I sent him."[5]

One of the most striking instances of Annie's power, however, is recorded by Elizabeth Stuart Phelps in her autobiography, *Chapters from a Life*, where she reveals that it was Annie who decided to publish *The Gates Ajar* (1868). Phelps notes that she had sent the manuscript to Ticknor and Fields and had not had a response for two years. "I have the impression," she wrote, "that the disposal of the book . . . wavered for a while upon the decision of one man, whose wife shared the reading of the manuscript. 'Take it,' she said at last, decidedly; and the fiat went forth."[6] *The Gates Ajar* was a runaway best-seller, and became something of a national cultural phenomenon: there were *Gates Ajar* souvenirs, even reportedly a *Gates Ajar* cigar. Phelps had high praise as well for James Fields, noting that "he was incapable of that literary snobbishness which undervalues a woman's work because it is a woman's" (147).

While Annie's editorial judgments may have been crucial to the success of many women writers, it was not primarily as a manuscript critic that she had her influence. Rather it was as a personal friend and hostess that she had her greatest effect. Annie established the Fieldses' home on Charles Street as a kind of literary salon. Most of the literary lions of the day—including Hawthorne, Longfellow, Holmes, Emerson, Whittier, Dickens, and Arnold—were at one time or another entertained there. While the edited materials she left for posterity present the image of a proper Bostonian lady (this is especially the case with Mark A. DeWolfe Howe's 1922 selections from her diaries, *Memories of a Hostess*), it is clear that her success as a hostess lay in a warm and lighthearted personality. Henry James, for example, speaks of her having a "capacity for incapacitating laughter."[7] In a little-known letter Harriet Beecher Stowe wrote to George Eliot one senses the atmosphere Annie Fields was able to create. After playfully scolding Eliot for making *Middlemarch* so lofty and sober, Stowe invited her to visit America and stay with Annie Fields. "We want to get you over here, and into this house, where, with closed doors, we sometimes make the rafters ring with fun."[8]

We have noted the intensity of Annie's friendship with Rebecca Harding Davis and Harriet Beecher Stowe. That she had a similar bond with Celia Thaxter, the New Hampshire poet, is evident in numerous letters from Celia to Annie. One reads: "If I could only see you every week and clasp your hand and look into your faithful beautiful eyes, everything would be easier to bear."[9] Fields also formed a close tie with another poet, Louise Imogen Guiney, to whom she bequeathed a portion of her estate.

But undoubtedly the most important of her relationships was with Sarah Orne Jewett. The two met probably in the early 1870s. Sarah was then at the beginning of her career, and published her first major work, *Deephaven*, with Osgood & Co. in 1877. By the time James Fields died in 1881 their relationship had intensified. In succeeding years they formed a couple, and spent much of the year together, sometimes at 148 Charles Street, sometimes at the Fieldses' summer home in

Manchester-by-the-Sea, Massachusetts, sometimes at Jewett's home in South Berwick, Maine, and sometimes on extended travels, including four times to Europe. They formed what used to be called a "Boston marriage," that is, a marriage-like commitment formed between two women.[10] Scores of letters remain attesting to the intensity of their bond.

After Jewett moved in, 148 Charles Street became a veritable mecca for up-and-coming women writers. Among those making the pilgrimage were Mary Noailles Murfree ("George Craddock"), Alice French ("Octave Thanet"), Mary E. Wilkins (Freeman), Edith Wharton, and Willa Cather. Mary Murfree's 1885 visit to Boston was particularly memorable to all concerned, for they had expected "George Craddock" to be a man. In his recollections William Dean Howells acknowledged that he was among the most surprised, for he prided himself on being able to recognize a feminine writer by her style and by her script. "The severely simple, the robust, the athletic hand which she wrote would have sufficed to carry conviction of her manhood against any doubts."[11]

Murfree published her first major work, *In the Tennessee Mountains*, in 1884; it was a collection of local color stories set in the southern mountains. Sarah Orne Jewett had been much impressed by a story, "The Star in the Valley," and wrote her an appreciative letter on May 19, 1884. Murfree later allowed that Jewett was her favorite author and that in her family circle they had often read her works aloud (Parks, 180).

Alice French, a midwestern local colorist, was born in Andover, Massachusetts, in 1850, at a time when Elizabeth Stuart Phelps (then a child) was living there. In 1852 Harriet Beecher Stowe also moved to Andover; she and her husband, Calvin, who was affiliated with the Andover Theological Seminary, lived near the French family. Alice moved from Andover to Iowa when she was five years old, so it is unlikely she formed any lasting relationship with either Stowe or Phelps at this time.

Rather, once again, it was Jewett who appears to have been the primary influence. Like Jewett, French formed a "Boston marriage" with Jane Crawford, with whom she lived much of her life. French made the pilgrimage east in 1899, when she visited both Jewett and Mary E. Wilkins. In 1907, near the end of her life, Jewett wrote a candid letter to French urging her to live up to her great potential. The letter includes a fairly direct critique of French's novel *The Lion's Share*, which Jewett saw as pandering to popular taste. She urged French to leave "this sort of thing to others who can't write anything else." She went on: "You can show the causes of things in your country—leave the surface effects to people who see no deeper. . . . I have a sense of your standing in the middle of a country waiting to be written about."[12]

Jewett was right, of course, but the person who would bring that midwestern country to life was not Alice French. It was Willa Cather, another young Midwesterner, who made the pilgrimage to 148 Charles Street to meet her acknowledged mentor in the fall of 1908. Jewett counseled her protégée, in advice similar to that which she gave French, to write about what she was familiar with—her "Nebraska life."[13] This advice fortunately fell on receptive ears. The first novel Cather wrote about Nebraska and under Jewett's influence was *O Pioneers!* (1913), an acknowledged masterpiece. It is dedicated to Jewett.

Cather has given us one of the most vivid descriptions of the Fields–Jewett salon in her essay "148 Charles Street." Once again one has the impression of an awe-stricken aspirant trembling in the presence of by this time near-legendary greats. Cather claimed she recognized Jewett from her picture on the "Authors" card game that she had played as a child. Cather corroborates other observers' sense of Annie Fields's merriment but notes that it was combined with an extensive but unpretentious knowledge of literature and art. At the age of seventy-four, Cather found, Annie was still abreast of the latest cultural happenings.

She was not, as she once laughingly told me, "to escape anything, not even free verse or the Cubists!" She was not in the least dashed by either. On, no, she said, the Cubists weren't any queerer than Manet and the Impressionists were when they first came to Boston, and people used to run in for tea and ask her whether she had ever heard of such a thing as "blue snow," or "a man's black hat being purple in the sun!"[14]

What most impressed Cather about "Mrs. Fields" was that "she rose to meet a fine performance, always—to the end. At eighty she could still entertain new people, new ideas, new forms of art" (71).

Jewett's effect on Cather was profound. Cather has detailed it in several pieces, most notably her essay "Miss Jewett" and a little-known newspaper interview printed in 1913.[15] From a series of three hitherto unpublished letters that Willa wrote Jewett in 1908 it is clear that Jewett's encouragement of the young writer came at a critical point in Cather's life. The latest of these, dated November 18, is an eight-page tightly spaced epistle written from Cather's Greenwich Village apartment. In it she notes that her boss, S. S. McClure, ". . . tells me that he does not think I will ever be able to do much at writing stories. . . . I sometimes, indeed I very often think that he is right." She complains, however, of the "deadening" effect her newspaper work is having on her, and wonders whether she ought not take some time off to devote to her writing. She concludes by noting that she has recently reread Jewett's classic story "Martha's Lady" and that while it is humbling to a novice, it nevertheless "makes [her] willing to begin all over."[16]

It is undoubtedly in response to this letter that Jewett wrote her famous letter of December 13 that encourages Cather to distance herself from the newspaper world, to find her "own quiet centre of life, and write from that . . . to the human heart, the great consciousness that all humanity goes to make up."[17]

Earlier Jewett had gently criticized Cather's inauthenticity in using a male persona in "On the Gull's Road," a story that appeared in the December *McClure's*. Cather had brought it to her attention with trepidation: "I am afraid you won't like it, dear Lady. The scent of the tube-rose seems to cling to it still."[18] Cather well knew Jewett's distaste for artificiality in literature, and her preference for authentic realism.

Edith Wharton also visited Fields and Jewett. On one occasion in 1905 she motored up to Jewett's home in South Berwick. This was shortly before the publication of *The House of Mirth*, Wharton's first major novel. On other occasions she visited them both at Charles Street.[19] One of Jewett's oldest friends, Sara Norton, became a close friend to Edith Wharton, which undoubtedly created another connection between the two. One Fields letter mentions Norton's visit to her, which was to be followed by a visit of several days with Wharton.[20]

Wharton acknowledged that she saw Jewett and Freeman as her "predecessors" in the field, but said she hoped to write works more realistic than those produced "through the rose-coloured" vision of these women.[21] It is my contention, however, that not only were Jewett's and Freeman's works far from "rose-coloured" but that Freeman's vision, especially, came close to Wharton's own (see chapter 8).

Other linkages among the women of the local color school can also be specified. Usually, as noted, these were through the agency of Annie Fields. In September 1884 Annie and Sarah took an excursion south to

Connecticut, where they visited Harriet Beecher Stowe in Hartford. On the way back they dropped by Rose Terry Cooke's home in Winsted. Cooke unfortunately was out, and in a letter dated September 28 wrote how she regretted missing them.[22] Jewett had evidently left a note at the Cooke house (it is dated the same day) articulating her admiration for Cooke's work: "I never have expressed myself about that noble story of the Reverend Tucker or indeed anything I have read and loved of your writing."[23] The story Jewett refers to is "Some Account of Thomas Tucker" (*Atlantic Monthly* August 1882, *The Sphinx's Children*, 1886).

Cooke had been a regular contributor to the *Atlantic* from the very first issue in 1857; it included her "Sally Parson's Duty." She had corresponded with the Fieldses for many years, beginning probably in 1861 when he began as editor and when Cooke's "Miss Lucinda" was published. Letters between Annie Fields and Jewett indicate that Cooke visited at Charles Street and that Annie kept abreast of her news. Annie mentions at one point Rose's "sad tale" that her husband's father had failed in business; he had "lost all his money and some of hers."[24]

Annie's and Sarah's 1884 journey had also included a somewhat more momentous visit with Harriet Beecher Stowe in Hartford. Stowe was at the end of her long writing career, and while she did not die until 1896, her last decade was not a working one. The visit apparently ended a short rift between Annie and Harriet over some criticism Stowe had made of Annie Fields's poetry. More important, however, was the meeting between Stowe and Jewett, who, as Stowe's biographer put it somewhat dramatically, "received the torch of New England realism from Harriet Beecher Stowe's hand" (Wilson, 623). Jewett had brought Stowe her latest novel, *A Country Doctor* (1884), to which Stowe responded in a letter dated September 24 that she found it "not only interesting and bright but full of strong and earnest thought" (624). She invited Fields and Jewett to visit her in Florida the next winter.

Jewett had admired Stowe's work since childhood. On several occasions she noted how influential Stowe's novel *The Pearl of Orr's Island* (1862) had been on her. In her 1893 (Second) Preface to *Deephaven* Jewett noted:

It was, happily, in the writer's childhood that Mrs. Stowe had written of those who dwelt along the wooded seacoast and by the decaying, shipless harbors of Maine. The first chapters of *The Pearl of Orr's Island* gave the younger author of *Deephaven* to see with new eyes, and to follow eagerly the old shore paths from one gray, weather-beaten house to another where Genius pointed her the way.[25]

In a later letter Jewett stressed again her enthusiasm for the novel, noting that she still found it "just as clear and perfectly original and strong as it seemed to me in my thirteenth or fourteenth year, when I read it first." However, she noted that Stowe was not able to sustain the "noble key of simplicity and harmony" throughout the work and that it remained incomplete.[26] In an even later, unpublished letter Jewett recanted this criticism and returned to her earlier enthusiasm: "I take back [my belief] that the last half of the book was not so good. . . . I still think that she wrote it, most of it at her very best height." She mentions further how much she appreciates the book's "heroines," especially Sally Kittridge.[27] (*The Pearl of Orr's Island* is discussed in chapter 4.)

The publishers of the *Atlantic* celebrated Stowe's seventieth birthday (actually it was her seventy-first) with a garden party on June 14, 1882. In attendance were the usual assemblage of literary notables, including *Atlantic* contributors Rose Terry Cooke and Elizabeth Stuart Phelps. Annie Fields and Sarah Orne Jewett were on their first trip to Europe. Years later, however, they attended Stowe's funeral in Andover, where Annie put a sprig of purple flowers on the coffin.

Stowe had known Rose Terry Cooke from birth.[28] Their paths crossed occasionally, since they were both natives of Connecticut and spent many years there (Cooke, her entire life). Rose Terry Cooke graduated from the Hartford Female Seminary in 1843. The school had been founded in 1823 by Harriet's sister, Catherine Beecher, who was its director until 1831. Harriet herself attended and taught at the school from 1824 to 1832. Harriet and Rose had the same influential instructor, John Pierce Brace, who advocated a liberal philosophy, and who is the model for Jonathan Rossiter in Stowe's *Oldtown Folks*.[29] Cooke was well known by many members of the Hartford Nook Farm community where Stowe lived in the latter years of her life. Undoubtedly literary influences passed mutually between Stowe and Cooke.

Harriet also had a decided influence on Elizabeth Stuart Phelps, as the latter notes in her autobiography. As a child Phelps had been entertained by Stowe, and Stowe's youngest daughter had been a schoolmate (*Chapters*, 134–35). Not only were they neighbors in Andover, but Stowe provided for Phelps a "model of female success." For, as one critic of Phelps points out, ". . . she too was a woman who made her novels into sermons advocating the reformation of social ills and urging the recognition of human needs."[30] Phelps called Stowe "the greatest of American women" in her autobiography and mentions visiting Stowe in her Florida home, where she sought advice on her poetry (*Chapters*, 136). This was in 1874. In 1873 Phelps had asked Stowe to sign a petition urging dress reform for women.[31] More than any of the others Stowe and Phelps, as daughters of theologians, were touched by the shifting theological winds of the time. Calvin Stowe, Harriet's husband, was for a time a colleague of Austin Phelps, Elizabeth's father, at the Andover Theological Seminary.

Elizabeth married Herbert Dickinson Ward in 1888. Ward's family was from Jewett's hometown, South Berwick, but the new Ward couple apparently never lived there. Late in her life Phelps contributed to a composite book, *The Whole Family* (1908), to which Mary E. Wilkins Freeman also contributed a chapter.

Jewett and Fields knew Elizabeth Stuart Phelps well; they corresponded with her and met with her occasionally. A series of letters exchanged between Jewett and Fields makes it clear, however, that Jewett, at least, had considerable reservations about Phelps's later work. This was despite the fact that each had admired her earlier work. We noted Annie's decision to publish *The Gates Ajar*. Sarah mentions in her 1869 diary having read aloud to her grandmother Phelps's story "Kentucky's Ghost"—"which I like so much." She also read *The Gates Ajar* the same year.[32]

But Jewett found fault with Phelps's *The Story of Avis* (1877). While "it interested me very much as Miss Phelps's books always do," she found Avis an improbable character, and therefore feared the book would do more harm than good. "Avis is far too exceptional a character." Highly idealistic figures like Avis had little effect on the reader; she was "beyond . . . most people's comprehension, or without their observation."[33] This suggestive comment not only shows how much of a realist Jewett was at heart; it also shows that the rationale behind her realism was a belief that inflated characters or rhetoric did not serve one's cause, in this case the cause of women. Only realism could do that. (*The Story of Avis* will be discussed in chapter 6.)

A later letter shows that it was also Phelps's extravagant style that

Jewett found distasteful. Annie protested to Sarah that "Jack the Fisherman," a story by Phelps published in June 1887 (in *Century*), was "a great story"—"whatever strictures one may have about E. S. P." And: "I have seen nothing like it—it is absurd to talk of faults of style—they may be as thick as blackberries but the grand spirit is there."[34] It is evident, therefore, that Jewett had had some discomfort with Phelps's style.

The reverse was also the case. In an extant letter from Phelps to Jewett, probably written in 1886 or 1887, the former criticizes Jewett's "quiet and finished touch" and suggests in a veiled way that Jewett should choose more lively topics for her stories. "When you brought Mrs. Fields the roses there was a red one hidden among the protecting white. *Once*—the day I met you—I saw the flash of the red rose in your face." Phelps further suggests that Jewett should treat "the red red rose" sometime in her work.[35] While this passage itself should serve to indicate what Jewett disliked in Phelps's style—its sensationalist artificiality—Phelps's criticism of Jewett's work is not without merit. Jewett never addressed personal or socially relevant topics in the overt way Phelps did (with the possible exception of *A Country Doctor*), and if Phelps is suggesting that she deal fictionally with her relationship with Annie Fields, one wishes that Jewett had heeded the advice (although one may certainly read aspects of that relationship in many of Jewett's works, especially *The Country of the Pointed Firs* and "Martha's Lady").[36]

Mary E. Wilkins Freeman was never an intimate of the Fields–Jewett circle, but she nevertheless met with them on various occasions, and exchanged correspondence. A cordial letter from Freeman to Jewett written probably in 1899 thanks Jewett for returning something and notes: "My little reunions with you always warm my heart, and I wish they came oftener."[37] Letters between Freeman and Fields concern invitations to Charles Street.[38]

Jewett and Freeman admired one another's work. Freeman read Jewett as an apprentice writer. Jewett sent Freeman an admiring note after the publication of Freeman's first volume of stories, *A Humble Romance and Other Stories*, in 1887. To this Freeman responded, "I never wrote a story equal to your 'The White Heron.' I don't think I ever read a short story, unless I except Tolstoy's 'Two Deaths,' that so appealed to me."[39] Jewett later acknowledged that she found Freeman's "An Object of Love" to be "a model of short fiction."[40]

Freeman's affiliation was less with Houghton Mifflin and the *Atlantic Monthly*, which published much of the other local colorists' material; her publishing house became Harper's and many of her stories appeared in *Harper's* or in *Harper's Bazar*.

It was Mary Louise Booth, editor of *Harper's Bazar*, who first "discovered" Freeman. She published her "Two Old Lovers" in the magazine in 1882. Freeman and Booth soon developed a strong relationship. Several letters remain which document the strength of Freeman's affection for Booth. She signed her letters to Booth with a nickname, "Pussy Willow," and almost always expressed her love for the older woman. Booth helped her get some of her early stories into shape. In two letters Freeman noted how she had drastically revised "A Wayfaring Couple" according to Booth's suggestions.[41] Since this story, as we have it, remains a masterwork (see chapter 8), one can only assume that Booth's editorial suggestions had been astute.

On December 5, 1905, Harper's held a birthday celebration in New York City for one of its most distinguished authors, Mark Twain. It was his seventieth birthday. Among scores of notables in attendance was Mary E. Wilkins Freeman, by then at the peak of her fame. Also there was a younger writer who was yet to make her mark, Willa Cather. Only missing to make the event of symbolic significance equal to the Holmes breakfast was the presence of Edith Wharton. For the purpose of neatness, it would be nice if others in the emerging generation of women writers, such as Ellen Glasgow and Mary Austin, had also been there. But they were not, and therefore the event is not quite the landmark in women's literary history as the Holmes breakfast. Nevertheless, as Wilson might have put it, the torch of women's literary realism was passed in the first decade of the twentieth century from the New England local color school to a new generation of women writers.

4

Harriet Beecher Stowe and the Emergence of a Female Arcadia

Harriet Beecher Stowe pioneered the women's tradition of local color realism in this country. Several of the stories later collected in *The Mayflower; Or, Sketches of Scenes and Characters Among the Descendents of the Pilgrims* (1843) are among the first authentic American pieces of local color literature. That is, they depict authentic regional detail, including authentic dialect, authentic local characters, in real or realistic geographical settings. Moreover, several of these early Stowe stories carry on the traditions of women's literary realism noted in previous chapters: they are antiromance, they critique inauthentic female behavior, and they posit the rural locale as a site that nurtures genuinely sensible and assertive women.

Stowe once noted that she saw "Chaucer's Griselda as a false ideal of womanhood."[1] What she meant by that becomes clear when we study the statements she made about Lady Byron, whom she saw as the prime example of oppressed womanhood and whose cause she took up in 1869. In an article and later a book Harriet made the then-shocking revelation that Lord Byron had committed incest with his half sister and that Lady Byron had borne this odious knowledge in silent shame to her death. That Stowe emphatically rejected such silent suffering as a proper mode for women is clear in a letter she wrote to Horace Greeley, editor of *The New York Tribune*, dated December 19, 1869, eliciting his support: "I consider Lady Byron's story as a type of the old idea of woman: that is, a creature to be crushed and trodden under foot whenever her fate and that of a man come in conflict." Stowe further maintains that Lady Byron was a greater genius than her husband: "Had she been in a man's form, she might have controlled and guided the thought of England; but all has been wrecked, crushed, hidden, in her history as wife of a wicked reprobate. Her life was a silent sacrifice."[2]

On the other hand, Stowe did rely on a variation of the Cinderella script in some of her early stories, and did present stereotypically sentimental female characters in some of her early novels. Yet from the beginning Stowe favored strong, assertive, competent women characters in her fiction, and was a consistent supporter of women's rights in her nonfiction.

She advocated rights for women in a series of articles devoted to the issue in the late 1860s. The earliest of these appeared shortly after the Civil War in the *Atlantic Monthly*'s "Chimney-Corner" column, which Stowe wrote under the pseudonym Christopher Crowfield. (Stowe's occasional use of male pseudonyms and male narrators was undoubtedly done to lend authority to her voice, but it must be acknowledged that the device is hardly a feminist one.) The November and December 1865 columns address the "woman question." In these Crowfield advocated the central ideas of the nineteenth-century women's rights movement, including the right to vote. Another set of articles, published in 1869 in *Hearth and Home*, was also devoted to the topic. She argued that "taxation without representation is tyranny" and urged that since women were taxed they deserved the right to elect their representatives (*Hearth and Home* 28 August 1869). She demanded married women's property rights and opposed unfair divorce laws (*Hearth and Home* 7 August 1869). She ridiculed the vapid occupations to which leisure-class girls were socialized (*Hearth and Home* 19 June 1869), and lamented women's unequal educational opportunities (*Hearth and Home* 16 January 1869). Stowe further urged that women be allowed to enter any profession they may be suited for.

We see nothing unfeminine or improper in a woman's exercising the right of suffrage; we see no impropriety in her pursuing an extended career of study, which shall fit her to be a physician, we think women may be architects [or] . . . landscape-gardeners [or] . . . teachers of a naval school . . . in short there is no earthly reason why they should not . . . use every advantage which God and nature have put in their hands.[3]

Stowe's affiliation with the women's rights movement ended, however, when a personal conflict developed between her and that eccentric free-love advocate Victoria Woodhull in the early 1870s over Woodhull's allegation that Harriet's brother, Henry Ward Beecher, a celebrated minister, was having an affair with a parishioner, Elizabeth Tilton. This scandal dragged on for several years, culminating in a trial in 1875 in which Beecher was sued by Theodore Tilton for alienation of affection; it ended in a hung jury. The net result of this sensation on Harriet's work was that she retreated from her earlier profeminist position and presented increasingly weaker models of womanhood in her social novels of the 1870s.[4] These included *My Wife and I* (1871), *Pink and White Tyranny* (1871), and *We and Our Neighbors* (1875). Her final local color works, *Poganuc People* (1878) and *Sam Lawson's Oldtown Fireside Stories* (1881), while entertaining, are essentially reworkings of material she had used more effectively earlier in her career. This analysis will, therefore, focus on her early pioneer stories and on her local color novels, *The Minister's Wooing* (1859), *The Pearl of Orr's Island* (1862), and *Oldtown Folks* (1869).

Harriet Beecher Stowe's first published story—"Isabelle and Her Sister Kate, and Their Cousin" (*Western Monthly* 2 February 1834)[5]— is in the satirical vein of the Edgeworthian novel of manners, and involves a critique of the romantic heroine, construed as an empty-headed flirt, or "belle" type. But it also includes a Cinderella plot in which the plain, sober sister Kate is rewarded with the prince, in this case Cousin Edward.

Stowe opens her story with the by-then conventional rejection of romance. She announces that she is not going to use the stereotypical "heroine" for her protagonist. "I am not about to choose this angel for my heroine, because she is . . . too much like other heroines for my purpose." Rather Stowe chooses the ordinary sister, in a move that clearly reflects a realist's impulse. The narrator of the story is a Stowe persona, and although it is not entirely clear whether the voice is male or female, it seems to be a woman "very much like the reader." This device—that of the narrator speaking conversationally to the reader as to a neighbor—was one Stowe was to use quite effectively throughout her career, though in her later works she often employed male personae as narrators.

Stowe's next story, originally published as "A New England Sketch" (*Western Monthly* 3 April 1834) and included in the *Mayflower* collection as "Uncle Tim," is the first that can fairly be labeled local color. It too opens with an antiheroic, antiromance address to the reader:

And so I am to write a story—but of what, and where? Shall it be radiant with the sky of Italy? or eloquent with the beau ideal of Greece? Shall it breathe odor and languor from the orient, or chivalry from the occident? or gayety from France? or vigor from England? No, no, these are all too old—too romance-like—too obviously picturesque for me. No, let me turn to my own land—my own New England.[6]

Here, as elsewhere, Stowe associates the romance with exotic, foreign worlds. Instead she proposes to write about what she knows, "one of those out of the way places where nobody ever came . . . a green little hollow, wedged like a bird's nest between half a dozen high hills." The plot of this story is insignificant, but it does include characters with regional names (Patience Mosely, Comfort Scran), and authentic details of rural New England existence, and the use of regional dialect. The New England locale is, however, very general.

The narrator's attitude toward the material is already that of the insider who nevertheless takes a stance of comic irony toward her subjects, and whose very awareness that the characters are speaking in a dialect that is not her own standard English reflects a self-consciousness and a sense of irony well beyond that of a naive "insider." This peculiar insider–outsider narrative stance is characteristic of the local color school; its significance becomes more noteworthy in later writers.

"Cousin William," another *Mayflower* story, opens with yet another striking manifesto against the sentimental romance.

Now we know that people very seldom have stories written about them, who have not sylph-like forms, and glorious eyes, or at least "acertain [sic] inexpressible charm diffused over their whole person." But stories have of late so much abounded, that they actually seem to have used up all the eyes, hair, teeth, lips and forms necessary for a heroine. . . . These things considered, I regard it as fortunate that my heroine was not a beauty. She looked neither like a sylph, nor an oread, nor a fairy; she had neither "l'air distingué" nor "l'air magnifique," but bore a great resemblance to a real mortal girl.[7]

Mary, the central figure, is accomplished in traditionally female occupations but also is an intellectual who is forthright and assertive.

The other stories in the *Mayflower* collection comprise a potpourri of themes and types. "Old Father Morris. A Sketch from Nature" is another local color piece that entails a Yankee commoner who speaks in dialect. "Little Edward" also has a vague New England setting, as does "Love *versus* Law." Nearly all of the stories have a pointed moral, following in the vein of Maria Edgeworth's *Moral Tales*, which many authorities suggest as the most important literary influence on the young Harriet. "The Tea-Rose" and "The Sempstress" urge compassion for the poor. "Let every Man Mind his own Business" is an early temperance story. "Love *versus* Law" has a pacifist message.

In her Preface to the *Mayflower* collection Harriet's sister, Catherine E. Beecher, notes that it was the effect of Maria Edgeworth and Sir Walter Scott that made novel-reading, much less novel-writing, permissible in their strict religious household. These works were acceptable because they had an ostensibly moral purpose. Indeed, Stowe's biographer notes that the only fiction the young Harriet was exposed to was Edgeworth's *Moral Tales* (along with Cotton Mather's *Magnalia*). One of her earliest memories (and one of the few of her mother) was of being read Edgeworth's story "Frank" in 1816 (Wilson 39, 51).

One suspects that the Edgeworth influence was not confined to the Irish writer's moral stories. For, as we have seen, the very concept of local color literature owes much to her, as does the antiromance theme so central to women's realism. Both of these ideas were essential ingredients in Stowe's early fiction.

Two other early Stowe stories continue the criticism of the superfluous flirt seen in the first story. "The Only Daughter" (*Godey's Lady's Book* March 1839) concerns the domestication of a flighty aesthete into a responsible homemaker. "The Coral Ring" (*Godey's* June 1848) urges that a young woman ought to do something with her life other than just being a "parlor ornament." She should exert herself in the public sphere: promote temperance, speak out on religious issues, visit and tend "the poor." Here, incidentally, is a literary corroboration of Barbara Berg's thesis that leisure-class women turned to charity work to deal with their own feelings of anomie, and that the women's rights movement developed in part out of this experience.[8]

"The Deacon's Dilemma; or the Use of the Beautiful" (*Independent* 22 November 1860) is an early feminist story that concerns an oppressed wife. Her husband has forbidden her to have a flower garden because it is not useful. The wife is too "meek" to protest, but chafes inwardly. "The poor woman had a kind of chronic heartsickness . . . but she never knew exactly what it was she wanted." The plot resolves when their son takes up her cause and convinces the father he has erred. This story anticipates Mary E. Wilkins Freeman's "The Revolt of 'Mother.'" Stowe depicted oppressed wives in several other works, notably Crab Smith's wife in *Oldtown Folks* and Molly Molloy, a battered wife in *My Wife and I*.

The most significant of Stowe's early stories, however, is "A Yankee Girl" (*The Token and Atlantic Souvenir* 1842).[9] This story shows most forcefully Stowe's ideal of womanhood, and, while it follows a "euphoric heroine's text"—that is, it concerns a proper rejection of seduction—the protagonist is competent and assertive, and therefore realistic far beyond the prototypes of the Cinderella model. Mary Parsons of northern New Hampshire is the tale's main character. She presents an androgynous amalgam of gender traits: "In her you shall find the union of womanly delicacy and refinement with manly energy and decision, womanly ingenuity and versatility in contrivance, with manly promptness and efficiency in execution" (62). There is something very American about this story. One senses the influence of the frontier, perhaps mediated through the writings of Caroline Kirkland, with whose work, as we have noted, Stowe was familiar.

Mary is the opposite of the romantic heroine. For one thing she is American and, therefore, in Stowe's eyes, she is down-to-earth and practical. Following Edgeworth, Stowe negatively associates artificial manners forced upon women with the European establishment and with the upper classes. Mary is a commoner, a democrat, and has a natural competence and unpretentiousness. "She learns early to make energy and ingenuity supply the place of wealth. Born in a land where all are equal, no princess could surpass her in the feeling of self-respect" (62–63). She has "a cool, easy air, a freedom and nobility of manner," a "form" kept fit "by constant and healthful exercise." And: "Even at the wash bench, our heroine, in her neat, close fitting calico, never looked so little like a lady as some fair ones we have seen in curl papers and morning gowns . . ." (65).

The plot is that Mary has the common sense to reject the seduction designs of a European aristocrat and rake who happens to pass her farm. Instead, in another version of the two-suitors convention,[10] she chooses sensible, hardworking American George, who is going to raise himself by his bootstraps by going to college. She rejects the Earl of Beresford in terms that call for a marriage of equals: "If I ever marry, it will be one who can fully appreciate the affection I give . . . and not one who will always look upon me as a sort of ornamental appendage to his station . . ." (70). Mary, unlike many a stereotypical romantic heroine, successfully outwits the would-be seducer and makes her own decisions.

Stowe's sympathies for the oppressed scarcely need documentation. Yet it is important to understand that she saw America, and particularly rural New England, as the place where the once-oppressed lived freely as equals, in natural if humble surroundings. These were the people she identified with. And *"against* us," she once asserted, are "all privileged classes, nobles, princes, bankers and great manufacturers, all who live at ease."[11] In her New England novels one finds the earliest extended description of a precapitalist, preindustrial matriarchal community—a topos characteristic of the New England local colorists. It is drawn as a counter to the urban, upper-class, capitalist, industrial, male-dominated civilization that they saw as inimical to their survival as free women, and to the survival of the natural, rural world they loved so well, and which was their refuge.

The Minister's Wooing (1859), the first of these novels, is in many ways a brilliant work. It opens, significantly, with a chapter entitled "Pre-Railroad Times." But the central concern of this novel is with the repression and oppression of women by patriarchal systems. The most important of these is Calvinism and in particular its theses of preordination and eternal damnation of the unconverted. The women in the novel reject Calvinism, presenting a variety of reasons for their position. One woman in particular, Mrs. Merwyn, is severely repressed by her Calvinist faith until she is converted to an essentially female religion, one that is liberal, compassionate, tolerant, and accepting. There is also a woman, Madame de Frontignac, who is a victim of European high-society mores, in particular the wiles of an oily seducer. She too is saved by the other women. Calvinism is seen as an abstract, alien, and male system that is not indigenous to this New England village. It is the village women who voice what is seen as the natural, compassionate ethic of the area. Most strikingly in this novel one sees an opposition drawn between an oppressive alien patriarchal system that comes somehow from abroad the village, and the simple, real, free rural world.

The novel's plot concerns the courtship of Mary Scudder, the "heroine," by two men—one of whom is a rather stuffy minister, Dr. Hopkins, whose views, while not strictly Calvinist, are nevertheless highly abstract and inhuman. The other suitor is James Merwyn, an attractive but irreligious youth, who is thought, for a while, to be lost at sea. Since he had not converted, it was held (in the Calvinist view) that his soul was eternally damned. The point is finally rendered academic when the boy returns, alive, to marry Mary.

In the meantime, however, the substance of the novel transpires in the development of various women characters and their anti-Calvinist positions. Perhaps the most forceful of these is Candace, the Merwyns' black slave. Candace is clearly based on Sojourner Truth, a celebrated women's rights activist, whom by this time Stowe had met.[12] Candace has a central speech in the novel that is modeled on Truth's famous "Ain't I a Woman?" speech of 1851. When her owner decides to find out if his slaves really want freedom (this novel is set at the turn of the eighteenth century), Candace declares emphatically, "When Gineral Washington was here, I hearn 'em read de Declaration ob Independence and Bill o' Rights; an' I tole Cato den, says I, 'Ef dat ar' true, you an' I are as free as anybody.' It stands to reason. Why, look at me—I a'n't a critter. . . . I's a reasonable bein'—a woman,—as much a woman as anybody."[13]

Candace's feminist sentiments are also to the point. Her owner had once told her to be more deferential to her husband, Cato, because "the wife is the weaker vessel" (101). Candace responded with incredulity. "'*I* de weaker vessel?' said Candace, looking down from the tower of her ample corpulence . . . 'I de weaker vessel? Umph!'" (101). The narrator notes that "a whole women's-rights' convention could not have expressed more in a day than was given in that single look and word" (101).

It is Candace who presents the most cogent argument against the Calvinist idea of natural depravity: ". . . nebber did eat dat ar' apple . . . Don't tell me!" Thus she rejects the idea that "all men sinned in Adam" (78). Candace's ideas are rooted in a common-sense realism. She rejects a foreign pretentious illogical philosophy in terms that derive from her own sense of everyday reality. Once again we see at work the fundamental dialectic of the early novel: the common person debunking upper-class "educated" pretensions.

But other women in the novel also reject such impositions. Mary, in many respects the stereotypical "angel" of the sentimental romance, has a visceral reaction against the notion of eternal damnation. Stowe's narrator observes: "Where [male] theorists and philosophers tread with sublime assurance, woman often follows with bleeding footsteps; women are always turning from the abstract to the individual, and feeling where the philosopher only thinks" (15). Mary's faith is rooted in her own existential feelings—not in a learned system. It was her "womanhood—that vivid life in the soul and sentiment" that resisted "the chills of analysis" (164).

Miss Prissy, the town's seamstress and one of the first of the long line of New England spinsters to grace local color literature, is also anti-Calvinist. Her ethic is refreshingly practical. In discussing whether James went to heaven or not she allowed that "as the Doctor says, 'amiable instincts a'n't true holiness,' but then they are better than unamiable ones." And: "Now I know we can't do anything to recommend ourselves to the Lord, but then I can't help feeling some sort of folks must be by nature more pleasing to Him than others" (209). Prissy is a pivotal figure in the novel because she arranges the marriage between Mary and James when everyone else is stymied as to how to disengage Mary from the minister. Prissy simply tells Hopkins that Mary still loves James. Candace calls this "one o' de bes' day's works you eber did in your life!" (307)—an obvious endorsement of a free-will salvation-by-works philosophy.

Cerinthy Ann Twitchel is another minor character who rejects damnation. She has said that "she never should get reconciled to Decrees and 'Lection, 'cause she can't see, if things is certain how folks is to help 'emselves." Her mother, one of the few female supporters of the Calvinist position, retorts, "Cerinthy Ann, folks a'n't to help themselves, they's to submit unconditional" (25). Mary's mother, the Widow Scudder, also pays lip service to Calvinism, though she doubts whether certain of Mary's behavior is evidence of grace, as Hopkins suggests, thinking it may be only "natural sensibility" (205).

Mrs. Merwyn is the figure most victimized by Calvinist theory. She goes nearly berserk trying to adjust to the idea of her son James's eternal damnation. Finally she rebels, saying, "Mary, I cannot, will not be resigned!" (193), and she accepts the simple, New Testament, "feminized" version of Christianity suggested by Candace and the narrator.[14]

The story of Madame de Frontignac has little to do with the anti-Calvinist theme but much to do with Stowe's feminist assertions against decadent "foreign" mores that victimize women. Madame was unhappily married to an older man who treated her "as a beautiful, though somewhat absurd little pet" (131). In her unhappiness she has fallen in love with an unctuous seducer, Aaron Burr. "Gentle and pliable as oil, he seemed to penetrate every joint of the menage by a subtle and seductive sympathy" (152). Madame de Frontignac, however, wishes to escape her decadent aristocratic past. She wants to reject her "Madame" self with all its vanities and retain only her pure, natural, "Virginie" self. She is "tired of the balls, and the dancing, and the diamonds, and the beaux" (217). She also wants to reject Burr, and to this end enlists Mary's aid.

Mary and Virginie themselves develop a very romantic attachment. At one point Virginie puts her head on Mary's lap, saying ". . . how I love you!" Later the two frolic on the seashore. Madame "would laugh at her, kiss her, gambol round her, dress her hair with fantastic coiffeurs, and call her all sorts of fanciful and poetic names . . ." (261). Unfortunately Burr arrives, somewhat symbolically, to disrupt this idyl. Madame sees New England as a "true Arcadia" (276).

Thus, while *The Minister's Wooing* has in the past been seen as having significance for its forceful rejection of Calvinism, one may see that, couched in the continuing traditions of women's realism, it concerns rejection of patriarchal systems that pervert and destroy women's potential. That the realistic setting is turned into a female Arcadia is a local color topos we have seen developing as early as Maria Edgeworth.

The tension between sentimentalism and realism in Stowe's work is most evident in the second of her local color novels, *The Pearl of Orr's Island* (1862). This is the novel that so influenced Sarah Orne Jewett, but, as Jewett herself pointed out, it is not flawless. Its composition took place over nearly a decade and it lacks a sense of integral unity. As Jewett comments, "Alas, that she couldn't finish it in the same noble key of simplicity and harmony; but a poor writer is at the mercy of much unconscious opposition. . . . The result is a divine touch here and there in an incomplete piece of work."[15]

There are, however, continuing threads in the work. One is that the setting remains constant and is the most realistic of Stowe's literary environments. Indeed, she drew from "living studies," as she herself acknowledged when she began work on the piece in 1852. "There is 'old Jonas,' my 'fish father,' a sturdy independent fisherman-farmer, who in his youth sailed all over the world. . . . I must go to Orr's Island and see him again." As Forrest Wilson comments, ". . . our first realist had to have models in her work; she knew no other way of writing" (300–301). This is to be sure a slight exaggeration, but Orr's Island was and is a real place off the coast of Maine near Brunswick, where Harriet had spent the years 1850–52 during which time she wrote and published *Uncle Tom's Cabin*.

But, while the context of the work is that of local color realism with its authentic details of character, dialect, and locale, the plot remains a sentimental romance in the tradition of *Charlotte Temple*. It concerns two children—a girl, Mara, and a boy, Moses—who are orphaned by two separate shipwrecks off the coast (highly improbable occurrences, needless to say). Each exemplifies stereotypically female and male traits, respectively. Moses is an early example of the machismo male; he is aggressive, morally insensitive, and uncontrollable. Mara is the opposite: passive, finely strung, hyperemotional. The plot is a Charlotte Temple plot; the girl Mara dies of consumption, which event effects a conversion of the evil male to more humane, civilized behavior. Moses is revealed to have come from a wealthy, decadent, foreign family—once again evidence of Stowe's notion that male tyranny is not indigenous to her idyllic New England.

Moses is a very Byronic figure, which leads one to suspect that Stowe's awareness and concern about Lady Byron's plight had become injected centrally into this novel. Stowe met Lady Byron, nee Anne Isabella Milbanke, three times during the writing of this work: in 1853, 1856, and 1860. It is likely she learned the "true story" of Lady Byron's suffering during the 1856 visit.[16] Though their meetings were brief, their relationship had quickly developed a considerable intensity. In an 1857 letter Stowe wrote Lady Byron: "I left you with a strange sort of yearning, throbbing feeling; you make me feel quite as I did years ago, a sort of girlishness quite odd for me."[17] One historian, James C. Austin, suggests that "her infatuation" with Lady Byron was overpowering.[18] It is clear that Stowe's obsession with vindicating this symbol of women's oppression stayed with her for years. It undoubtedly does much to explain the plot of *The Pearl of Orr's Island*. For Moses, the Byron of the piece, is brought to his knees in repentence at the end and Mara enjoys the final spiritual triumph. Thus, despite the stereotypical nature of the plot, Stowe appears to have derived it from a real situation.

One particularly dramatic episode shows Moses' essential immorality as opposed to the fundamental virtue of the girl. It concerns a nest of eagles' eggs that Moses is determined to rob. Mara protests, "But the poor birds,—do hear 'em scream. Moses, don't you suppose they feel bad?" Moses responds with characteristic brutality: "I wish I had a gun now, I'd stop those old eagles' screeching."[19]

Katherine Jobes has suggested in a perceptive article that this scene provided the germ for Sarah Orne Jewett's story, "A White Heron," in which a young girl similarly defends her rural sanctuary against a foreign male intruder who would destroy it.[20] Indeed, the episode is archetypal of the fundamental dialectic one may note in women's local color literature: that of women identifying with their pastoral world against the male-controlled urban establishment. Both Moses in *The Pearl* and the male hunter in "A White Heron" represent an encroaching male imperialism.

Significantly, too, throughout local color literature women are more in tune with nature and have great sympathy for animals. Stowe in fact once wrote a passionate defense of animal rights ("Rights of Dumb Animals," *Hearth and Home* 2 January 1869). Elizabeth Stuart Phelps was a leader in the antivivisection movement and wrote several novels and articles for its cause. Jewett was a member of the Maine Society for the Prevention of Cruelty to Animals. Animals play meaningful roles throughout these women's fiction. Mary E. Wilkins Freeman devoted two volumes to a study of the interrelationship between animals, plants, and humans (*Understudies* and *Six Trees*).

The Pearl of Orr's Island is characteristic of the local color movement in other ways as well. Sally Kittridge, the other central female in the work, is clearly of a different stripe than Mara. She is competent and practical (she can drive her own carriage), energetic and active. And though she is something of a flirt, at least she can hold her own with Moses. Other characters are even more typically New England: Zepheniah and Mary Pennel, Captain and Mrs. Kittridge, the Reverend Sewell and his sister, Emily, and especially Aunt Ruey and Aunt Roxy. The latter are spinster sisters, humorously presented as eccentrics who take snuff but who are the unofficial arbiters of community life. "Miss Roxy was the master-spirit of the two, and, like the great coining machine of a mint, came down with her own sharp heavy stamp on every opinion her sister put out" (22). "She was one of those sensible, practical creatures who . . . if we shiver at them at times, as at the first plunge of a cold bath, we confess to an invigorating power in them after all" (23).

It is, however, *Oldtown Folks* (1869), that is the finest of Stowe's local color novels; it is indeed, in my view, the culminating masterpiece of her career. The work is narrated by Horace Holyoke, a figure who is supposedly based on Harriet's husband, Calvin Stowe. The work purports to be Horace's (or Calvin's) reminiscences of his childhood in Natick, Massachusetts; but it is not simply factual autobiography.

Like all fiction it takes its place in a continuing literary tradition, and like all fiction it is the result of the author's own process of selection and arrangement. The themes that concerned Harriet in earlier works are continued in *Oldtown Folks*. The Natick of the novel becomes a kind of feminist Utopia where women are freed once and for all from the tyranny of the "heroine's text," where women have at last lives of their own. The fact that Harriet excluded much of Calvin's material from this novel and used it later in *Sam Lawson's Oldtown Fireside Stories* is testimony to the fact that she had certain controlling themes in mind for the novel to which the excess material did not pertain. And, indeed, there is no unifying thread in the later *Fireside Stories*; it is a scrap bag, although entertaining, of leftover material.[21]

Oldtown Folks opens with a "preface" by Horace Holyoke in which he enunciates the classic realist narrative doctrine, that of mimesis. He claims he has attempted to hold a mirror up to nature and to reflect what he saw as faithfully as possible with little interpretation or moralizing. "In doing this work, I have tried to make my mind as still and passive as a looking-glass . . . and to give you merely the images reflected there."[22] Furthermore: "My studies for this object have been Pre-Raphaelite,—taken from real characters, real scenes, and real incidents." Pre-Raphaelitism, a nineteenth-century movement in painting, advocated a return to the principles of early Italian art—that of faithful detailed reproduction of nature. "I myself," Horace continues "am but the observer and reporter, seeing much, doubting much, questioning much, and believing with all my heart in only a very few things" (iv).

The world, however, that Horace remembers or rather that Stowe creates is once again an idyllic land where people—especially women—are allowed to grow freely to develop their strengths and competencies. But it is a world destroyed by the onslaught of capitalist industrialism.

"For that simple, pastoral germ-state of society is a thing forever gone.
. . . The hurry of railroads, and the rush and roar of business that now
fill it . . . have prevented that germinating process" (421). Nevertheless, such an environment was a perfect one to grow up in; indeed a
central theme of the work is "to show how the peculiar life of old Massachusetts worked upon us, and determined our growth and character
and destinies . . ." (261).

This statement shows how far Stowe had moved from any notion of
Calvinistic predestination. Rather it is one's environment, indeed one's
education and the quality of child-rearing, that shape the adult. Harriet derived some of these ideas from the pedagogical theory of her sister Catherine. Catherine, who wrote her own refutation of Calvinist
determinism in *The Elements of Mental and Moral Philosophy* (1831),
had founded her Hartford Female Seminary on the liberal notion that
one trains not only a person's mind but also her character. This "in
1830, in Calvinistic Connecticut . . . smelt of heresy. How could you
train character, when everyone's character had been foreordained
. . . ?"[23] Heresy or no, it was an idea which Harriet by 1869 fully accepted. By then, of course, Darwinistic notions of environmental influence were in the air and undoubtedly also had some effect on Harriet's
thinking.

One of the central causes Stowe advocates in *Oldtown Folks* is, therefore, proper, liberal child-rearing practices and educational institutions. She also urges that women's perspectives, which she sees as generally more humane, compassionate, and realistic than men's, be
included in patriarchal social institutions such as religion and higher
education. She attacks Calvinism once again, this time from the point
of view that it fails to include women's realities:

. . . woman's nature has never been consulted in theology. Theologic systems
. . . have, as yet, been the work of man alone. They have had their origin . . .
with men who were utterly ignorant of moral and intellectual companionship
with woman, looking on her only in her animal nature as a temptation and a
snare. Consequently, when, as in this period of New England . . . theology
. . . began to be freely discussed . . . it was the women who found it hardest to
assimilate it, and many a delicate and sensitive nature was utterly wrecked in
the struggle (438).

When the young male protagonists go off to college—to Harvard—
they find it deficient in women's knowledge. Harry notes: "the fact is, a

man never sees a subject thoroughly until he sees what a woman will think of it, for there's a woman's view of every subject, which has a different shade from a man's view." And: "It is confoundedly dull without [women]; these fellows are well enough, but they are cloddish and lumpish" (510–11).

Oldtown Folks is a world of few men and many, strong women. The men who exist are either tyrants (Crab Smith) or incompetent (Sam Lawson and Horace's father). Sam Lawson is an amusing, if ineffectual, "village do-nothing" who drifts around, telling tales and helping children and animals. Interestingly, Sarah Orne Jewett adopted her own nickname, "Pinney Lawson," in part after this character, perhaps because of his position as village raconteur but also probably because of his indolence, a trait she lamented in herself.

The women in the novel are diverse but for the most part strong and triumphant. The village matriarch is Grandmother Badger, a monumental figure who takes Horace in after his parents die. She "was . . . a tower of strength and deliverance . . . [She] belonged to that tribe of strong-backed, energetic, martial mothers . . . who fearlessly took any bull in life by the horns . . ." (18). Despite her apparent ferocity, and despite the fact that she is an adherent of Calvinism, she is warmhearted and opens her home to all strays. She believes in a free and open kind of child-rearing and is sensitive to animals. She objects to calf-killing as an "abominable cruelty" and says if she had her way we would not "eat creatures" (170).

The plot represents a momentous break with past sentimentalist patterns of women's fiction, and charts new ground. Unlike the typical sentimental/domestic novel, this work does not confine itself, solipsistically, to the fate of one pathetic character, but rather traces the lives and interconnections of a score of fascinating people.

The plot concerns the arrival of two orphaned children in town, and their education to adulthood. As in the typical sentimental novel, the children's mother has been a "seduced-and-abandoned" victim of their father, "a worthless, drunken, dissipated fellow." Stowe relates that "this poor woman had been through all the nameless humiliations and agonies which beset helpless womanhood in the sole power of such a man" (89). He had induced her to leave England and to come to America with him, but once there had abandoned her, destroying their marriage certificate—a plot strongly reminiscent of that archetype of the genre, *Charlotte Temple*. It is indeed as if Charlotte's children had somehow wandered away from the evil European tyranny of their father and into the benign, liberated world of rural New England. However, their almost mythical journey is not without obstacles.

First, the children—Tina and Harry Percival—fall into the hands of another worthless male, Crab Smith. Crab has tyrannized over his poor wife for years, she was "more properly speaking, his life-long bond-slave" (86). The narrator divagates to meditate on the question of wives' oppression: "Why half the women in the world marry the men they do, is a problem that might puzzle any philosopher; how any woman could marry Crab Smith, was the wonder of the neighborhood" (86). And then: "Worn to a shadow,—little, old, wrinkled, bowed,—she was still about the daily round of toil, and still the patient recipient of the murmurs and chidings of her tyrant" (87).

The arrangement is made that Harry is to stay with Crab, and Tina to go with Crab's sister, Asphyxia, who turns out to be too harsh a taskmaster, raised in Calvinistic ways. She has had a hard life: she had been a school-teacher, "and while she did the duty of a man, received only the wages of a woman"—an inequity, the narrator informs us, that persists (117).

The children, however, plot to escape, and do so successfully, arriving finally at the home of Grandmother Badger. Tina is adopted by Mehitable Rossiter, a town spinster, and Harry remains at the Badgers'. Mehitable is a firm believer in lenient child-rearing, which works well for hypersensitive Tina. Mehitable, another partaker of snuff, is the last in an old aristocratic line but is a "faithful and true," unpretentious person. She is troubled, nevertheless, and notes in a letter to her brother that men can expunge their depressions "by sea voyages and severe manual labor. A *man* can fight this dragon as a woman cannot. We women are helpless,—tied to places, forms, and rules,—chained to our stake" (214).

Another of the reasons Mehitable is depressed is that her rebellious sister, Emily, has run off to Europe and become a devotee of Rousseau and a free-love philosophy. This was because she had been brought up under a severe and harsh Calvinist regime that proved too much for her sensitive, gentle nature. She had, while in Europe, been abandoned with child by a heel named Ellery Davenport. After this misfortune Emily acidly commented, ".   the world, of course will approve *him* and condemn *me*" (581). As the plot unfolds, Tina marries Ellery, not knowing of his past, only to learn of Emily's existence after the wedding. Tina insists, however, that Emily and her daughter be supported financially. But shortly thereafter Ellery is conveniently killed in a duel, so Tina is free to marry Horace, the narrator, and live happily ever after.

Another important woman figure in the novel is Esther Avery, "the leading scholar" in Greek and Latin at the Rossiter Academy, where the children are sent for secondary school. Stowe labels this world "Cloudland," an obvious Utopian reference. Esther is an androgynous figure, "the MAN-WOMAN . . . who unites perfectly the nature of the two sexes" (439). She had the "strong logical faculties . . . which are supposed to be the characteristic of man." She also had, nonetheless, female "moral perceptions" and "intuitions." But "Esther never could have made one of those clinging, submissive, parasitical wives who form the delight of song and story . . ." (439). Esther's only flaw is a tendency toward too much cerebral activity, which Stowe thinks is unhealthy. Esther eventually marries Harry Percival, however, in a presumably egalitarian union.

Also at the school is Miss Nervy Randall, the Rossiter's housekeeper, who believes (with Sojourner Truth) "that if women want any rights they had better take them, and say nothing about it" (426). In her youth Nervy had navigated a ship across the ocean after the captain, her brother, had fallen ill. She knew Greek and Latin, and counseled students in mathematics as well, made her own butter and dried her own herbs. She is one of the first models in literature of a happy single woman. She "was about the happiest female person whose acquaintance it has ever been my fortune to make," says narrator Horace. "She had just as much as she wanted of exactly the two things she liked best in the world,—books and work. . . . As to station and position she was as well known and highly respected . . . as the schoolmaster himself" (427). Nervy is one of the earliest of those local color originals that constitute one of the charms of the genre.

There is a complaint in the novel that women do not receive an education fully equal to men's. "As a general rule," the narrator notes, "the country academies of Massachusetts have been equally open to both sexes." The only exceptions were Andover and Exeter, the most prestigious. He acknowledges that "the classics and higher mathematics were more pursued by the boys than the girls." But if a girl wished to do so, "there was neither cherubim nor flaming sword to drive her away" (422). At the Rossiter school, however, girls had to learn certain female accomplishments such as embroidery, but this is seen by the narrator as a "characteristic of the ancient *régime*" (423). The boys lament that the girls cannot go on to college with them. Harry notes that Esther was "by far my superior . . . in both Greek and mathematics; and why should she not go through the whole course with us . . .?" In the "Cloudland" of rural New England, by contrast, women had had equal educational opportunities.

Harriet Beecher Stowe furthered the development of women's literary realism by continuing and extending the critique of the stereotypical, male-identified heroine of the romance whose sole aim in life was to appear demure and weak, and thereby to ensnare a husband. Until her turnabout in the 1870s Stowe presented many original and strong women characters.

Moreover, she exhibited the same kind of provincial pride as Maria Edgeworth; in her case it was New England that became a kind of rural paradise, an Arcadia, where patriarchal tyrannies such as Calvinism were overcome, and where women were free to develop their potential and form strong friendships with one another. In retrospect, Stowe's vision of New England appears nearly Utopian, for in the writings of Rose Terry Cooke another and darker side of New England women's lives makes its appearance.

5

Rose Terry Cooke: Impoverished Wives and Spirited Spinsters

Born to an inheritance of hard labor . . . fighting with . . . the instinct of self-preservation, against a climate . . . rigorous [and] fatally changeful; a soil bitter and barren . . . without any excitement to stir the half-torpid brain, without any pleasure . . . the New England farmer becomes in too many cases a mere creature of animal instincts . . . hard, cruel, sensual, vindictive. . . . And when you bring this same dreadful pressure to bear on women . . . the daily dullness of work, the brutality, stupidity, small craft, and boorish tyranny of husbands, to whom they are tied beyond escape, what wonder is it that a third of all the female lunatics in asylums are farmers' wives?[1]

In these tragic terms Rose Terry Cooke, in her story "The West She-tucket Railroad," characterized the miserable lives of rural New England women in the nineteenth century. How far we are from the sentimental romance. How far even from the comparatively Utopian vision of Harriet Beecher Stowe. The best of Cooke's stories exhibit this kind of grimly authentic realism. At times her vision anticipates that of the naturalists: a bleak, uncompromising view of humanity, and particularly of men, as dull brutes. Of the local colorists only Cooke and Freeman reach this level of realism. Cooke may well have had a direct influence on Freeman, for many of Cooke's most powerful stories were published in *Harper's* in the 1880s—just at the time when Freeman was beginning to publish, also in *Harper's*.

Not all of Cooke's work is, however, of this caliber. Indeed, Cooke's progress as a writer is erratic; her literary production, which includes nearly 200 stories, is inconsistent, ranging from derivative Sunday-school moral tales to strange romantic fantasies to some of the finest literature produced by the local color school. This study will focus on her local color works.

Cooke created a fictional universe analogous to Stowe's rural New England and Edgeworth's rural Ireland. As with her predecessors', Cooke's Connecticut is a moral centrum, a kind of ideal community where characteristically local people go about their daily business. Like her predecessors Cooke consciously rejected romance conventions (though she erred, herself, occasionally in the direction of sentimentalism) and she produced critiques of the "belle" and the rake. Like Stowe she was decidedly opposed to Calvinist tyrannies (recall that she was educated in Catherine Beecher's Hartford Female Seminary) and she presented a world where strong women thrive. Usually they are spinsters. In several stories Cooke revealed a suspicion of urban civilization (in this case, New York City) and clearly believed that purity of heart and strength of character were nourished in the rural village.[2] But Cooke did not seem to have the same resistance to industrial progress as the others; indeed, in "The West Shetucket Railroad" she suggests that the railroad may be a boon to the region in that it is breaking down the isolation of rural farmers' families.

Where Cooke differs from her predecessors, however, is in her acknowledgment of the depth of evil that exists even in the rural world and in her refusal to attribute that evil to foreign influence. As the opening citation indicates, Cooke fully realized that evil could be homegrown; indeed, she perceived that it may be fostered by the bareness and hardness of New England's physical environment. For Cooke the worst conditions were often found within a marriage.

Cooke carried further the critique of Calvinism offered by the Beecher sisters by urging that the repressions occasioned by harsh religious strictures, combined with the brutal hardships forced by the environment, created people who were impoverished economically, emotionally, and spiritually. With Rose Terry Cooke the romance of the idyllic New England village is over, and while versions of it persist in Jewett and Phelps, it is Cooke's vision that comes to prevail in women's literature: in the works of Freeman and later in Edith Wharton's classic study of New England, *Ethan Frome*.

Several of Cooke's stories are set in the same place, though its name may vary, and the same characters reappear in several stories, so that even though obviously not written in sequence, they present a kind of continuing saga of Connecticut village life. Four of her early stories are set in Cranberry. These were all published in *Putnam's Monthly* and include her first important published story, "The Mormon's Wife" (*Putnam's* June 1855), which is narrated by a Parson Field, who tells his own story in "Parson Field's Experience" (*Putnam's* April 1856). "Love" (*Putnam's* March 1857, *Huckleberries Gathered from New England Hills* 1891) and "Joe's Courtship" (*Putnam's* May 1857) are also set in the same locale and include some of the same characters. Many of Cooke's thematic concerns and stylistic characteristics are evident in these early stories.

"The Mormon's Wife" is the first of many Cooke stories to deal with the oppression of wives in marriage. While Stowe touched on the subject, Cooke came to be nearly obsessed with it, although, ironically, she never endorsed the women's rights movement, which she criticized in some of her stories. Nevertheless, the oppression of wives is a dominant Cooke theme. In "The Mormon's Wife" the evil is attributed in Stowe fashion to exotic foreign mores; the story also includes its share of trappings from the romance, including a shipwreck and an orphan. The plot is that an innocent orphan, Adeline, marries John Henderson, who adopts Mormonism, seen as a "delusion" by the narrator. After moving to Utah he takes two new wives—which is the beginning of the end for Adeline, whose heart then "turned to a stone" and who soon died of consumption. The betrayal by the husband and the emotional withering of the woman are typical Cooke themes. Adeline eventually realizes, "I should not have married him; it was an unequal yoke, and I have borne the burden." "Parson Field's Experience" also deals with a woman whose love is thwarted, in this case by misguided religious principles and male inattention, also perennial Cooke concerns.

The third of the Cranberry stories, "Love," is well-crafted and significant in many ways. It is one of the first to use what became a staple local color format: a group of locals sit around reminiscing as they perform some chore together. On this occasion they are sorting apples; often they are quilting or shelling peas. After some chitchat one of the characters is sparked to narrate the central story. In the case of "Love" it is Aunt Huldah Goodwin, a strong, down-to-earth, cheerful soul, who tells the story in dialect. This is Cooke's first use of dialect.

The story itself is unimportant, but the narrative style includes examples of one of Cooke's greatest achievements as a writer: her ability to forge metaphors drawn from authentic local detail, metaphors that are as indigenous to the personality as the locale. With this device, which Stowe used and which Jewett carried to the point of brilliance, the authentic integrity of the local color story was accomplished.

Aunt Huldah, for example, observes: "Lovin' some folks is jest like pickin' chestnuts out of the burr,—you keep a-prickin' your fingers all the time, and the more you try and keep on, the more it pricks" (*Huckleberries,* 238). Or:

But now she acted for all the world like my scarlet runner that Old Red trod acrost one day when the boys left the gate open, and crushed it down into the mud; and there it lay, kind of tuckered out, till one of the feelers got blowed against the pickets, and cotched hold, and lifted itself up, ring by ring, till the whole fence post was red with its blows, and covered with the green leaves (*Huckleberries,* 243).

Cooke's genius is, I think, evident in these passages; she is able to make universal comments about human nature through the use of metaphors drawn from her own environment, and yet appropriate to the speaker. Aesthetic consistency is a hallmark of great literature, and at her best Cooke created several masterpieces that can stand with the best of world literature. Indeed, this brilliant use of authentic imagery is one of the important distinctions one may make between the local colorists and the sentimentalists, whose figurative language was often trite.

In addition to the Cranberry stories Cooke wrote several set in Bassett, Connecticut. Most of these were published in *Harper's Monthly;* they include "About Dolly" (*Harper's* March 1877), "Squire Paine's Conversion" (*Harper's* March 1878, *Somebody's Neighbors* 1881), "Cal Culver and the Devil" (*Harper's* September 1878, *Somebody's Neighbors*), "Mrs. Flint's Married Experience" (*Harper's* December 1880, *Somebody's Neighbors*), "Miss Beulah's Bonnet" (*Somebody's Neighbors*), and "How Celia Changed Her Mind" (*Huckleberries*).

Another set of linked stories are those in which Polly Mariner, Cooke's great spirited spinster, appears as a character. Many of these were first published in the *Atlantic Monthly.* They include "Ann Potter's Lesson" (*Atlantic Monthly* September 1858, *The Sphinx's Children* 1886), "Lizzie Griswold's Thanksgiving" (*Atlantic Monthly* March

1859), "Polly Mariner, Tailoress" (*Galaxy* February 1870, *Somebody's Neighbors*), "Clary's Trial" (*Atlantic Monthly* April 1880, *Huckleberries*), and the aforementioned "How Celia Changed Her Mind."[3] A curious Indian woman, Moll Thunder, addicted to tobacco and alcohol, recurs in several stories, notably "Doctor Parker's Patty" and "Too Late" in *The Sphinx's Children* (1886), and "A Town Mouse and a Country Mouse" in *Huckleberries Gathered from New England Hills* (1891).

Cooke's uncompromising realism and her significance as a groundbreaker in women's literary realism can be best seen in the stories in which she documents the grim realities of marriage. The Cinderella myth meets its demise in these relentless depictions of what happens after the marriage vows are taken: there is no happy ending.

"The Ring Fetter" (*Atlantic Monthly* August 1859), subtitled "A New England Tragedy," is one of the earliest of these. The story, although set in western Connecticut, has some of the earmarks of the sentimental romance: an innocent whose parents have died, Mehitable Hyde, is courted and wed by an unscrupulous drunkard, Abner Dimmock. Unlike the earlier works, the story does not hinge on Mehitable's premarital chastity. That is not an issue. Rather the story concentrates on the marriage itself. The narrator consciously rejects the vision of the sentimentalists, who tend to fade out at the moment of marriage, considering it *the* happy ending. Rather, she notes, in a lengthy and rather sarcastic aside:

Here [at the wedding], by every law of custom, ought my weary pen to fall flat and refuse its office; for here it is that the fate of every heroine culminates. For what are women born but to be married? . . . But life, with pertinacious facts, is too apt to transcend custom and the usage of novel-writers; and though the one brings a woman's legal existence to an end when she merges her independence in that of a man, and the other curtails her historic existence at the same point, because the novelist's catechism hath for its preface this creed—"the chief end of woman is to get married"; still neither law nor novelists altogether displace the same persistent fact, and a woman lives [on] . . . when she binds herself . . . to another soul.

Mehitable Dimmock's postmarital fate is a grisly one. Her husband, as they are escaping from the law, kills their infant to silence it by throwing it under the wheels of their carriage. He later chains her up to keep her from escaping, which she nevertheless later does, only to commit suicide by drowning.

Another early story, which is probably Rose Terry Cooke's but which has been attributed to Elizabeth Stuart Phelps,[4] is "'Tenty Scran'" (*Atlantic Monthly* November 1860). This story, while not about wife abuse, is nonetheless an unromantic look at a failed courtship, an early adumbration of Sarah Orne Jewett's "A Lost Lover" and of Mary E. Wilkins Freeman's much anthologized "A New England Nun."

Content Scranton waits twenty years for her fiancé, Ned Parker, to return from sea. By the time he returns she has grown resentful: "Ned Parker! poor, selfish cre'tur', just playing with me for fun. . . . He let me know what kind of cre'turs men are. . . . I haven't had to be pestered with one all my life, I'm thankful." When she sees him she realizes how lucky she really is. He had become "a coarse, red-faced, stout sailor-like man, with a wooden leg . . . [who] swore like a pirate, chewed, smoked a pipe, and now and then drank to excess." Another character, Aunt 'Viny, who had brought up 'Tenty, is described as being "hard of feature, and of speech, as hundreds of New-England women are. Their lives are hard, their husbands are harder and stonier than the fields they half-reclaim to raise their daily bread from." There is nothing sentimental or romantic in Cooke's sharp view.

Cooke's indictment of male tyranny in marriage is presented most forcefully in three stories later included in her collection *Somebody's Neighbors* (1881): "Freedom Wheeler's Controversy with Providence" (*Atlantic Monthly* July 1877), "Squire Paine's Conversion" (*Harper's* March 1878), and "Mrs. Flint's Married Experience" (*Harper's* March 1880).

"Freedom Wheeler" is about the taming of a tyrant by the women who must deal with him—not before, however, his behavior leads to the death of his first wife, Lowly Mallory, "a feeble piece," who bears him child after child, all of them daughters except the first. He rejects the girls, hoping for another son. Aunt Hannah and Aunt Huldah, spinster sisters, see that Lowly's constant pregnancy and continual exhaustion are leading to her death. The narrator notes: "This is the life that was once the doom of all New-England farmers' wives; the life that sent them to early graves, to mad-houses, to suicide; the life that is so beautiful in the poet's numbers, so terrible in its stony, bloomless, oppressive reality" (331). Freedom, however, will not relent, and Lowly dies. His second wife, Melinda Bassett, is more than his match: "Land of Goshen," she announces, "do you s'pose I'm goin' to hev a man tewin' round in my way all the time, jest cos he's my husband? . . . I ain't nobody's fool, I tell ye, Aunt Hanner" (345). Melinda and the two aunts finally get Freedom under control.

"Squire Paine's Conversion" is somewhat similar to "Freedom Wheeler." Squire Paine is a Calvinist, capitalist tyrant and a hypocrite: he runs a store and cheats his customers. He too marries a meek woman, Lucy Larkin, in this case for her money. The narrator comments sarcastically: "Perhaps . . . Mrs. Paine . . . did not experience all that superhuman bliss which poets and romances depict as the result of matrimony—but then who does?" (103). The squire's "conversion" comes after he learns, mistakenly, that his daughter had been killed in a railway accident. When he learns she is alive, he repents.

The most powerful of these stories is "Mrs. Flint's Married Experience." The Widow Gold, who had lived in her daughter and son-in-law's home for the fifteen years since the death of her husband, longs to have her own home and husband, and so marries the only man available, hypocrite tightwad Deacon Flint. This turns out to be a serious mistake. Flint is a harsh tyrant. Her life becomes unmitigated slavery: ". . . she toiled on dumbly from day to day, half fed, overworked, desperately lonely, but still uncomplaining . . ." (395). Her predecessor, the deacon's first wife, had been "a silent and sickly woman, who crept about and worried through her daily duties for years, spent and fainting when the last supper-dish was washed. . . . She did not complain: her duty lay there . . . then she died. This is a common record among our barren hills, which count by thousands their unknown and unsung martyrs" (372–73).

Under the encouragement of two assertive spinsters, Mabel Eldredge and Polly Morse, Mrs. Flint, by this time barely alive, leaves her husband—in a plot that anticipates Freeman's less serious "The Revolt of 'Mother.'" However, in Cooke's story the community does not support Mrs. Flint's rebellion. In those days, the narrator tells us, "to find fault with authorities was little less than a sin, and for a wife to leave her husband, a fearful scandal. . . . Conjugal subjection was the . . . principle and custom . . ." (407). (Cooke occasionally sets evil ways in the past somewhat as Stowe roots them abroad. "Freedom Wheeler," for example, is subtitled "A Story of *Old* New England.")

The parish, therefore, demands that Mrs. Flint repent and return to her husband. With all the pressure, she is unable to present her side properly. "As in the case of many another woman, her terror, her humiliation, and a lingering desire to shield her husband from his own misdeeds, all conspired against her. Her testimony was tearful, confused, and contradictory . . ." (414). Polly and Mabel say they would far rather be single than endure such men, and attempt to shore her up. But Mrs. Flint, by now too beaten down to persist, recants only just before dying.

Occasionally Cooke turned the plot of the oppressed wife into a sentimental homily on Christian martyrdom. In these stories her point is that men are the crosses women must bear in order to achieve sainthood. Typical of these is "Saint the First" (*Root-Bound* 1885) and "One of Them" (*Independent* 20 November 1879). The latter is about Sarah Barton, who redeems her alcoholic husband through a kind of dogged masochism. When he roams the fields in a stupor, she would "follow him through swampy valleys and rock-strewn hills, her feet pierced and bleeding." One night "she rose up, and, lifting her husband in her arms, brought him home." Eventually her husband reforms: ". . . at last James crept up to his feet, lame for life, and weak as a man can be." This story is very much in the vein of the dominant American sentimentalist tradition analyzed by Helen Papashvily and Nina Baym, in which women enjoy spiritual triumphs over worthless men after enduring years of suffering (see chapter 2).[5] I mention it here to point up how very different Cooke's local color stories are from the sentimentalists'.

But, despite her occasional lapses into a kind of lachrymose Christianity, Cooke's dominant bent from her earliest stories is away from the hackneyed romance or sentimentalist conventions and toward authentic realism. In her first story published in the *Atlantic Monthly*, "Sally Parson's Duty" (which was in fact in the first issue of the magazine), Cooke debunks novelesque "heroines" by noting of her protagonist: "Sally was weeding onions in the garden,—heroines did, in those days." "Before Breakfast" (*Harper's* August 1860), another early story, also decries inauthentic fictional treatment of women. "The mass of men, and therefore the mass of novel-writers, puzzle their brains hopelessly over the nature of a woman, and finally describe her as a moral and religious doll." And "Poll Jenning's Hair" (*Harper's* October 1861, *Somebody's Neighbors*), while it presents a Cinderella plot, nevertheless opens with an antiromance preface: "It is sometimes a relief to have a story without a heroine, and this distinction alone can

I claim for mine. Nothing heroic or wonderful casts its halo about little Poll Jennings" (286).

Cooke's most succinct antiromance statement is in her opening to "Miss Lucinda" (*Atlantic Monthly* August 1861, *Somebody's Neighbors*), where she apologizes: "So forgive me once more, patient reader, if I offer to you no tragedy in high life, no sentimental history of fashion and wealth, but only a little story about a woman who could not be a heroine" (31).

Several of Cooke's early stories involve a critique of the "female quixote" or the "belle" type, or of the evil rake. As these topoi had become quite conventional by then I need only mention their titles. The belle is reformed in "Snip-Snap" (*Putnam's* March 1856), "Number Two" (*Harper's* September 1873), "How She Found Out" (*Galaxy* October 1875, *The Sphinx's Children*), "Will's Will and His Two Thanksgivings" (*Harper's* December 1879), and "Mary Ann's Mind" (*Huckleberries*). The coldhearted, manipulative rake is the target in "Martha Wyatt's Life" (*Harper's* May 1856), "The Assassin of Society" (*Harper's* May 1857), "Match-Making" (*Harper's* November 1859), and "Odd Miss Todd" (*Harper's* October 1882, *Huckleberries*).

"Clary's Trial" (*Atlantic Monthly* April 1880, *Huckleberries*) which brings to culmination Cooke's disposal of these romantic motifs, is a highly significant story. For, it combines a typical sentimentalist plot with a typical local color character, Polly Mariner. Polly intervenes in the seduction/abandonment script and saves the victimized woman from her fate.

The plot is set in a tavern on a turnpike between Hartford and Litchfield. Clary Kent is an innocent orphan who had been taken from the poorhouse at ten as a bound servant to Goody Jakeway, who ran the local tavern. Goody's son, Alonzo, is a sensualist rake who begins harassing Clary as she comes of age. Clary falls in love with him, and it looks as though marriage is imminent. Polly Mariner, the local seamstress, who is temporarily in residence at the tavern making shirts, discovers that Alonzo has a wife in England whom he deserted. Polly obtains a copy of the marriage license. In revenge Alonzo plants some property in Clary's trunk. When it is discovered, she is accused and later convicted of theft. Her sentence is a $100 fine or thirty lashes. Until she chooses, she must remain in prison. Polly manages to obtain the money just as the lashes are about to fall.

This is an important story when seen in the context of women's literary traditions, for the classic heroine's "dysphoric" text is interrupted by a New England spinster who outwits the would-be seducer and saves the girl. Polly's role in this story anticipates that of the eccentric female detective, such as Agatha Christie's Miss Marple, that later became so popular.

Cooke carried on the tradition initiated by Stowe of the powerful single woman character. Polly Mariner is perhaps the most notable example. Her own story is told in "Polly Mariner, Tailoress" (*Galaxy* February 1870, *Somebody's Neighbors*), one of the most popular of Cooke's stories.

Polly, left alone after her parents die, decides to learn a trade in order to support herself. Neighbors suggest that it would be more proper to live with relatives and work within their homes (for no pay). But Polly emphatically rejects this option: "Whilst I live by myself an' take care of myself, I a'n't beholden to nobody; and I know when my work's done, and what's to pay for't. I kin sing, or laugh, or cry, or fix my hair into a cocked hat, and nobody's got right or reason to say, 'Why do ye do so?' Fact *is,* I've got my liberty, 'n' I'm goin' to keep it" (233–34). The narrator rightly observes that had she lived later (the story is set around 1830), she would have been a prime mover in the women's rights movement. Polly's attitude implies, too, a clear rejection of Calvinist preordination. She believes that "folks's luck is generally their own makin'." Her behavior shows how people may shape their lives by their own decisions. She exemplifies a philosophy of free will and salvation by works, as do most of the spinster characters in local color literature.

One of the most powerful of Cooke's spinster stories is "How Celia Changed Her Mind" (*Huckleberries*). This story is also one of the most overtly critical of men and marriage. Set in Bassett, Connecticut, the plot concerns Celia Barnes, an orphan who had been bound out as "a white slave" to a "hard imperious woman" (288) until she reached eighteen; then she "apprenticed herself to old Miss Polly Mariner, the Bassett tailoress . . . and when Polly died, succeeded to her business" (289). She has rejected various unsuitable suitors; to one she said: "Ef you was the last man in the livin' universe I wouldn't tech ye with the tongs" (290).

However, she comes to envy the respect paid married women. "A woman that's married is somebody; she's got a place in the world; she ain't everybody's tag . . ." (284–85). Acting on her desires, she helps one young woman, Rosabel Stearnes, to elope, and then herself marries Deacon Everts. This is a mistake. "As her husband's mean, querulous, loveless character unveiled itself . . . she began to look woefully back to the freedom and peace of her maiden days" (307). "Now, admitted into the freemasonry of married women, she discovered how few . . . were more than household drudges . . . worked to the verge of exhaustion." Furthermore: "There were . . . some whose days were a constant terror to them from . . . intemperate brutes . . ." (308).

Celia learns that Rosabel's life has ended in this miserable fashion: in "poverty and malaria and babies" (310). She feels "almost like a murderess" when she learns of Rosabel's death. Soon her own husband, the deacon, dies—which elicits jubilation from her. After that, each year she turns Thanksgiving into a celebration for all the town old maids, and adopts two young girls, vowing to bring them up spinsters.

Another innovation in the treatment of women characters that Cooke pioneered was her recognition that women have feelings of passion, even sexual passion. Part, indeed, of her criticism of Calvinism was for the repression of passionate expression it enforced. In several of her early stories—"The Mormon's Wife," "Parson Field's Experience," "Martha Wyatt's Life," "The Assassin of Society"—women were depicted as victims of hardhearted or ignorant men who did not realize the depths to which the women's feelings went.

One of Cooke's stories about wild youthful passion concerns a love affair between two young women, "My Visitation" (*Harper's* July 1858). The narrator recounts an attraction she had for a sister boarder when she was in her teens. She notes that even in memory she "reeled" and "trembled with electric thrills" at the thought of this past adventure. Finally, after her friend Eleanor left her, a sober mature man courts her, but she feels that she has loved the woman too much to love a man. Eventually, however, she comes to appreciate his steadiness and they marry. Another story that has a homosexual subtheme is "Number Two" (*Harper's* September 1873). In it a Jonathan–David relationship develops between two men who work together in the western wilderness.

Women are often seen by Cooke as dying for lack of pleasure or entertainment. In "Uncle Josh" (*Putnam's* September 1857, *Somebody's Neighbors*), for example, a central female character, "Miss Eunice," languishes and dies from too Spartan an existence. She had "no recreation. . . . She did not know . . . that humanity needs something for its lesser and trivial life; that 'by all these things men live,' as well as by the word and by bread" (274). A curious early fantasy, "Maya, the Princess" (*Atlantic Monthly* January 1858), is a parable about the power of women's passion and how it turns bitter and destructive when not allowed an outlet.

Various minor characters in Cooke's work exhibit the damaging effects of emotional repression. In "The Forger's Bride" (*Lippincott's* March 1870, *The Sphinx's Children*) Mrs. Tyler, Sally's mother, keeps her heart like the front parlor, held in reserve. (One of Cooke's and Stowe's pet peeves was that people saved their front parlor room for guests.) Sally aches for the "deep, real love that lay hidden away in her mother's heart, very much as the best parlor and bed-room were shut up . . ." (326). "Odd Miss Todd" (*Harper's* October 1882, *Huckleberries*) suffers by falling in love with a younger man who jilts her. She struggles with jealousy and loneliness and "toward men . . . became pitiless and almost fierce" (120).

Probably the most intense tale of repressed passion is "Too Late" (*Galaxy* January 1875, *The Sphinx's Children*). Cooke set the story appropriately "in one of those scanty New England towns that fill a stranger with the acutest sense of desolation, more desolate than the desert itself, because there are human inhabitants to suffer from its solitude and listlessness . . ." (229).

Hannah Blair is brought up by very strict Calvinist parents, David and Thankful. Her mother has always withheld any expression of love for her child for fear of making of her an idol (a Calvinist injunction). Finally, however, Hannah and Charley Mahew fall in love and plan to marry. Moll Thunder, a local eccentric and a "born witch," predicts misfortune. Just before the wedding Hannah receives a mysterious letter that charges Charley had fallen from virtue. Under her strict religious code she therefore cannot marry him, and cancels the wedding at the last minute, refusing to see him. The agony of this decision is conveyed by the dying Hannah many years later to her daughter (she had later contracted a loveless marriage with another): "When he stood under my window and called me I was wrung to my heart's core. . . . I was upon the floor, with my arms wound about the bed-rail and my teeth shut like a vice, lest I should listen to the voice of nature"

(255–56). Hannah's confession—"I loved him so!"—has been elicited by the discovery that Charley died a lonely drunken pauper. The story is a clear indictment of the Calvinist will that denies the power of intense passion and ends by destroying people's lives. This becomes a central concern in the works of Mary E. Wilkins Freeman.

Cooke's opposition to Calvinism may be seen in several other stories. In "Mrs. Flint's Married Experience," as we have seen, a niggardly Calvinism is presented as a male tyranny that eventually destroys the woman. In "A Lay Preacher" (*Independent* 24 September 1874) Desire Flint, an orphaned servant girl, is seen as the true Christian in the household of a Calvinist theologian lost in doctrinal abstractions and low on charity. In "'Liab's First Christmas" (*The Sphinx's Children*) a mean-spirited farmer tyrannizes his meek, repressed wife, and refuses to allow any joy into their grim existence. After a brush with death, however, he repents and even acknowledges the value of the Christmas celebration.

Probably the most forceful indictment of Calvinism is in an early story, "Alcedama Sparks; Or, Old and New" (*Harper's* July 1859, *The Sphinx's Children*), which relates the generational transition from strict Calvinism to a more compassionate creed, a further example of the "feminization" of American religion.

Deacon Sparks, a straitlaced clergyman, has a wild-spirited son, Alcedama. Mrs. Sparks rejects the deacon's notion of infant damnation and human depravity and exhibits a liberal, tolerant philosophy of child-rearing. She is another of those hardheaded but compassionate matriarchs who populate local color literature, "no heroine of novel or story. . . . Not a particle of sentimentality tinged her nature. She neither screamed nor shrunk at a hoptoad. . . . She never cried all night over her own troubles or anybody else's . . ." (192).

The climax of the story occurs when Mrs. Sparks's parents, bankrupt and destitute, come to the area with their granddaughter, Hannah. The deacon refuses to take them in ("she made her bed, and she's got to lie on't . . ." [196]). So the family is auctioned off to the lowest bidder—a New England custom for dealing with welfare cases which Cooke compares to the auctioning of blacks in the South. Hannah too is "bound out" but the Sparkses hire her. Eventually, she and Alcedama fall in love, marry, and take in the old grandparents. A "new school" liberal minister takes over the local church, and the old regime has been vanquished.

Cooke's penchant for realism led her to present probably the most authentic view of women's lives yet to appear in literature. In her most significant stories she rejected the conventions of romance and sentimentalism, refused the Cinderella ending, and stuck to the grim, stubborn realities about poverty of means and spirit that characterized the New England scene.

With Cooke one notes a new ambivalence toward country life: on the one hand, there are the egalitarian villages like Bassett, centered in western Connecticut, where strong, active, usually single women work their positive ways; on the other hand, there is the recognition that women are dying on rural farms for lack of food, lack of love, and lack of freedom. This ambivalence will continue in the later local colorists, shaping the works of Phelps, Jewett, and Freeman.

6

Elizabeth Stuart Phelps: Burglars in Paradise

Elizabeth Stuart Phelps's literary career covered a span of nearly fifty years—from her first published story, "A Sacrifice Consumed," in 1864, to her death in 1911. During its course Phelps's moral vision of the realities of women's existence changed from an early assertive optimism to a resigned sense of the inevitability of male dominion. In this sense her career illustrates most dramatically the local colorists' transformation of women's literary realism from the kind of Utopian optimism about women's place seen in Harriet Beecher Stowe (and further developed by Sarah Orne Jewett) to the pessimistic ambivalence seen in Mary E. Wilkins Freeman (and later Edith Wharton) first adumbrated by Rose Terry Cooke.

Phelps's alteration may be seen as a transition from a fundamentally female-identified position to one that is male-identified. That is, she moved—both personally and in her works—from an attitude where her emotional and ideological identification was primarily with women to one in which that identification was with men. In this sense she may be said to have abandoned women's literary realism—as defined in the Introduction—in her late works.

It seems likely that Phelps's turnabout reflects the cultural transition, noted earlier, which began to occur in the latter nineteenth century. Several historians—in particular, Nancy Sahli, as noted—have stipulated the gradual emergence of a cultural disapprobation of close relationships between women and of women's exclusive commitments to women, their causes and issues. The reasons for this development are less clearly stated. Perhaps it was the movement of considerable numbers of women into institutions of higher learning that were almost exclusively male-oriented, or perhaps it was the growing popularity of various sexologists, including eventually Freud, with their inherent promotion of a patriarchal heterosexuality as the norm.[1] Perhaps it was simply a loss of heart over the mediocre results of the women's rights struggle.

In any event, by the early years of the twentieth century women had been thrust out of the naive, female-identified Eden of the Victorians. This was the "fall" Sahli referred to in her article. Two of Phelps's most important, if least attended, works similarly used prelapsarian imagery to suggest a fundamental change in women's estate. These were *An Old Maid's Paradise* (1879) and *Burglars in Paradise* (1886). Carol Farley Kessler has identified a similar transition in Phelps's novels from a belief in the possibility of female "self-actualization" toward an experience of "self-alienation."[2]

This study will follow the vicissitudes of Phelps's vision from the early feminist phase which continued generally until the 1880s, and which includes most of her powerful and innovative work, to her declining years, in which women's personal assertiveness and interpersonal inclination toward other women are put down in favor of conventional bourgeois marriage, with women in submissive roles. The culmination of these themes is to be found in a little-known but extremely significant story published in the last year of her life, "Sweet Home Road," discussed below.

The early Phelps, however, was a strong, courageous writer whose works, though they may be faulted for stylistic infelicities, nevertheless deserve a place in the evolving traditions of women's literary realism. Phelps's realism lies less in her interest in authentic local color locales—though she did root many of her works in such settings, especially in the Gloucester, Massachusetts, seacoast area where she lived for many years. Rather it is because she carries forward earlier conventions of women's literary realism that she merits inclusion in their ranks. Most significantly she continued, indeed brought to a sort of culmination, the female Utopia tradition in *An Old Maid's Paradise* (1879) and in her *Gates* novels: *The Gates Ajar* (1868), *Beyond the Gates* (1883), and *The Gates Between* (1886). In this series she popularized the anti-Calvinist sentiments of Cooke and Stowe and articulated most forcefully the tenets of a nonpatriarchal, "feminized" Christianity.[3]

Phelps differs, however, from her local color predecessors in several important ways. While she generally continues the repudiation of the Cinderella text in her early works (she falls back into the pattern in late

works), she is essentially a sentimentalist in her use of emotional hyperbole, her relative lack of humor, and in her relative disinterest in developing authentic local imagery, a hallmark of the other local colorists.
Moreover, the rural–urban tension seen in the others' works is less
marked in Phelps's, although personally she felt the conflicting attractions of Boston, as opposed to rural Massachusetts, in particular Andover, where she spent her youth.[4]

In Phelps's work the rural–urban division is seen more in terms of a
class conflict. Phelps is one of the first American writers to draw attention to the plight of industrial laborers, and some of her most memorable works dramatically depict their blighted working conditions.
Whereas the other women local colorists tended to identify their own
oppression with the oppressions of rural and ethnic groups (Edgeworth's Irish), Phelps and her characters took on the cause of the
urban proletariat. Like the other local colorists, however, she also had
an extraordinary empathy for animals. Several of her late works are
antivivisection tracts in fictional form.

Phelps, therefore, carried the social gospel of her mentor, Harriet
Beecher Stowe, into new areas, and carried a commitment to the
women's rights movement and to other social reforms much farther
than any of the other local colorists. Unfortunately, she was not able to
sustain these commitments, nor was she able to maintain or perhaps
she was not interested in maintaining a level of literary quality com-
parable to the best of the others.

Most of Phelps's early stories, those written in the 1860s, are insignificant sentimental pieces. There are, however, a few that are worthy of
note. Among these are several that describe strong, supportive relationships between women. "A New Year" (*Harper's* February 1865),
for example, is about two sisters who are alienated from one another.
Though they live together, they are bitter and dissatisfied, feeling that
life has passed them by. When one of them nearly drowns, however,
each comes to appreciate how much the other means to her.

"Cynthia, I want to tell you—" But Cynthia stopped her with a long, long
kiss . . .
". . . you have borne so much . . ."
"We've nothing left but each other," she said.

This was to become a typical Phelps plot pattern—near-death leading to a renewal of love—but in later works the renewal is almost always within a marriage.

Phelps's first story published in the *Atlantic Monthly*, "What Did She See With?" (August 1866, later entitled "What Was the Matter?" in *Men, Women and Ghosts* 1869),[5] is a woman's vision of transcendence: two women are united through the psychic powers of another woman. Marie and Alice are devoted sisters who have been separated. One day Marie writes Alice to come and live with her. Alice agrees to come, but on the way disappears, having apparently been killed in a railroad accident. Marie's servant, Selphar, a psychic, "sees" Alice in a western town; she is "*sick and in suffering*" (229). Marie goes West, fetches Alice, who is "bent and worn, gray-haired and shallow and dumb . . ." (230). After Marie gets Alice back home, Selphar discovers "the two women lying with their arms around each other's neck . . ."—a sight she is "glad" to have seen (231). This scene stands as a striking image of female unity and solidarity typical of Phelps's early work.

"At Bay" (*Harper's* May 1867) is another early story that describes a strong supportive relationshp between women. It also is one of Phelps's first works of social criticism and includes an important realist preface that pays tribute to Rebecca Harding Davis. Sarah, the narrator, is purported to be an uneducated country girl whose story has been printed unchanged by the editor. She asserts that the story of Martie Saunders's life, which she is about to tell, is a real one. So much of literature is not, she laments. "I often think when I have finished a novel, or a story . . . that it is strange why the people who make them up can not find something *real* to say. It seems to me as if I knew a good many lives that I could put right into a book, if only I had the words." One story, however, that she had found true to the lives of working people was "Paul Blecker," by the author of "Life in the Iron Mills." For: "It made you feel as if she knew all about you, and were sorry for you; and as if she thought nobody was too poor, or too uneducated, or too worn-out with washing-days, and all the things that do not sound a bit grand in books, to be written about." In this fashion Phelps redefines the anti-literary romance sentiment of the earlier local colorists to argue that new areas of reality be considered appropriate for serious literary treatment. This, of course, was already a well-developed trend, especially in England, where the so-called "industrial novel" was firmly established.[6]

Nevertheless, while "At Bay" is set in an industrial milieu, it retains many features of the old "heroine's text." Sarah is employed as a type-setter and rooms in Mrs. M'Cracken's boarding house. The story is about her roommate, Martie, an orphan, naive and innocent, who is hired as a compositor at the same company as Sarah. An intense friendship develops between the women. "After I was in bed . . . and we had lain a little while, I only stooped and kissed her softly on both her eyes . . . she threw her arms about my neck and broke out crying . . . 'It's been so long,' she said, '. . . since any body kissed me.'" Martie is sexually harassed at work by another worker, Job Rice (in a reworking of the evil seducer motif). When she refuses him, he spreads ugly rumors about her reputation. She is thrown out of the boarding house and nearly loses her job. However, her staunch refusal to marry him clears her name and she later marries a nice boy, David Brent. While this story obviously retains much from the sentimental romance, it does realistically depict the horrors of working-class existence for women, and it does show the strength of their mutual support. Women's primary commitment is still to one another.

Hedged In (1870), one of Phelps's first novels, continues in a vein similar to this story. It too deals with the urban poor, revolves around a strong relationship between two women, and includes prefatory assertions that this is to be a new kind of realism. "The inelegance of the figures may be pardoned if the reader will bear in mind that I am not writing 'a novel of high life.'"[7]

The novel is narrated by an outsider who speaks correct English, who comes to an urban slum area where people speak in dialect (once again the insider-outsider device commonly seen in local color works). There in a tenement filled with drunken women and babies she learns of Nixy Trent, a sixteen-year-old mother of a two-day-old infant. Nixy herself had been an orphan, out of a background of extreme poverty, had been abused, worked in a saloon, and became pregnant. In a stark reversal of sentimentalist views of motherhood Nixy hates her baby and contemplates killing it; the narrator is told that "a gal murdered her baby" in this place "years agone" (5). "We talk of 'instinctive maternal affection,'" the narrator continues, "I cannot learn that Nixy, when she left her child . . . experienced any other than emotions of relief" (57).

After wandering the streets, Nixy is taken in by Mrs. Purcell and her daughter, Christina. Nixy feels that had she had opportunities and been raised in a different environment she would be a different and a better person—Phelps thus continuing the liberal and un-Calvinist theory of character formation developed by the Beecher sisters, and auguring liberal and modern theories that attribute poverty to environmental deprivation as opposed to innate depravity.

Christina develops a fond affection for her new sister, Nixy, who blossoms in this matriarchal and nurturing environment. She is educated, and herself becomes the local schoolteacher. They begin calling her Eunice, more fitting to her new status. Finally, however, her past erupts. The townspeople cast her out when they learn of it. "The Scarlet Letter was upon her" (209). "Society had hedged her in on every side" (210). The Purcells stick by her, and Eunice reclaims her child, who dies shortly thereafter. Meanwhile, Christina decides to marry and move away. The event greatly disturbs Eunice, who dies on Christina's wedding day. This is one of the first adumbrations of the "burglars in paradise" theme—that of a man breaking into a happy female realm, which results in its destruction.

The Gates Ajar (1868), perhaps Phelps's most famous work, an all-time American best-seller, continues her emphasis on female solidarity. The theme of the work is similar to Stowe's *The Minister's Wooing;* its purpose is to resist and propose an alternative to Calvinist notions of the afterlife.

Mary Cabot, a twenty-four-year-old woman, has lost her brother in the Civil War. She cannot accept his death or be resigned to this fate, as she is supposed to, according to traditional theology. Once again the patriarchal representative of traditional Calvinism, Deacon Quirk, offers no consolation; indeed he only arouses her anxieties by raising the issue of whether the brother had died a professor of the faith, and therefore whether he had gone to heaven. Finally Aunt Winifred Forceythe arrives from Kansas, bringing her three-year-old daughter, Faith. Aunt Winifred is the voice of a compassionate "feminized" religion, heretical to the patriarchal system. Her view of heaven, which Phelps elaborates in *Beyond the Gates* (1883), is one of earth without evils. The dead retain their bodily form. They rejoin their loved ones in heaven, which in Winifred's view is much like a pleasant rural New England town with houses and pianos, brooks and trees.

Phelps herself noted that her motive in writing *The Gates Ajar* had been to provide solace for women who were grieving Civil War losses and who found none in the traditional pieties. "For it came to seem to me . . . that even the best . . . forms of our prevailing beliefs had nothing to say to an afflicted woman that could help her much. Creeds and commentaries and sermons were made by men. . . . [Doctrines] were chains of rusty iron, eating into raw hearts" (*Chapters from a Life,* 98). *The Gates Ajar,* therefore, is a culmination of the themes of sisterhood, of anti-Calvinism, and of the female Utopia that we have traced among the earlier local colorists.

Phelps wrote two other strong critiques of Calvinism: "Long Long Ago" (*Sealed Orders* 1879) and "The Reverend Malachi Matthew" (*Independent* 30 November 1882, *Fourteen to One* 1891).

An Old Maid's Paradise (1879), a nearly autobiographical novel, continues the image of a Utopian female sanctuary. Corona, a thirty-six-year-old "old maid," decides to move out of her brother and sister-in-law's home and build a home of her own. It is on the ocean front in Fairharbor (Phelps's fictional Gloucester). She moves in with a servant woman named Puella Virginia and a dog. Puella, like many of the local colorists' independent rural women, has little regard for men. When Corona suggests that they might have a man stay with them for protection, Puella says, "A—MAN!!! . . . What . . . two full-grown women— should want of *a* man."[8] It is a sentiment Puella will echo with less success in *Burglars in Paradise,* published by Phelps in 1886. Corona finds the independence, nevertheless, exhilarating; while out swimming she exults, "I am alive! alive!" (68).

Two women friends join them for a spell. The four women together form a kind of paradisiacal community. "Delicious to get out of the hot beach-dresses and down to the surf . . . and come to dinner with undried hair for which no one shall apologize, and . . . wander about the free, delightful, manless house" (139). "How perfect to be . . . four women by yourselves!" (139). Later Corona finds "she is intoxicated with . . . [her] existence . . ." (152).

Dr. Zay (1882), one of the earliest American novels about a woman physician, continues in a subtheme the idea of women being committed primarily to one another. Dr. Zay has chosen to practice in a rural area because the women there need women doctors. An observer notes that she is free from dependency on men, and at the same time does not forget her obligations to women.

"There are women that can't get through this valley without men folks. . . . If there ain't one round, they're as miserable as a peacock deprived of society.

. . . You know the kind I mean: if it ain't a husband, it's a flirtation; if she can't flirt, she adores her minister. I always said I didn't blame 'em, ministers and doctors . . . for walkin' right on over women's necks. It is n't in human nature to take the trouble to step off the thing that's right under foot. Now then! There are women that love women . . . care for 'em, grieve over 'em, worry about 'em, feel a fellow feeling and a kind of duty to 'em, and never forget they're one of 'em, misery and all."[9]

This is a clear statement of the distinction between a male-identified and a female-identified woman; the one devotes most of her time and energy to attracting the attention of men, the other feels an obligation to serve other women, seeing them as members of the same class.

This was, however, the high-water mark of Phelps's female-identified commitment. Already in *Burglars in Paradise* one may note a growing sense of discordancy. There is trouble between the two women characters, manifested as a growing class conflict. Corona puts down her servant's grammar and wonders, "Shall I lower to her level day by day?"[10] At the same time she becomes increasingly concerned about the threat of "burglars," and feels they may need male protection, an option Puella rejects. Eventually there is, however, a break-in. Worse from Puella's point of view is the fact that an old romance of Corona's also reappears. She reminds Corona that she, Puella, has turned down several suitors to remain with her. Corona reassures Puella that "the man doesn't live who could part me from you" (214). Nevertheless, the final line of the novel suggests that "the most dangerous house-breaker of all" may have "climbed up to Paradise," meaning that a male intrusion, welcomed by Corona, may well destroy the female realm.

Three late stories illustrate how far Phelps had fallen from her earlier female-identified ideals by the turn of the century. In "Twenty-four: Four" (*Harper's* January 1896, *The Empty House* 1910) two women live contentedly together; one is Mrs. Fortitude Fillebrown and the other her maid, Melissy Pulsifer. Like Puella Virginia in *An Old Maid's Paradise*, Melissy has little use for men, and in particular cannot understand Mrs. Fillebrown's nostalgia for her long-lost husband, who had been a drunkard and abused her. Melissy feels that "When a man ain't wuth it . . . he ain't *wuth*" (65). However, when the husband finally resurfaces, reformed, and the couple is reunited, Melissy seems to have been entirely forgotten by Phelps. What matters is the restoration of the marriage. In "Dea ex Machina" (*Harper's* January 1904) a woman physician is rebuffed for attempting to liberate an invalid wife;

her efforts are seen as an inappropriate disruption of the marriage.

Much more significant is "Sweet Home Road" (*Harper's Bazar* March–April 1910, *The Empty House*). In this story, a Doctor Cranfield and his daughter, Dremmer (nicknamed "Dream"), move to a country house where she falls in love with an invalid woman who lives next door. Phelps acknowledges the "unnaturalness" of the situation, a sign of her changed consciousness. "That this glamour should vibrate about an elderly, invalid woman . . . did not cause Dream any psychological surprises. Candidly, she would have preferred to adore a man, a young man. . . . But, for lack of the natural object of worship, she accepted the substitute deity, and her heart knelt to the unknown power" (292). Dream comes to worship the neighbor, Mrs. Meriden. "Every day had its projects of devotion, every hour its inventions of tenderness . . . she stood in her garden . . . choosing and culling votive offerings for her goddess"—whom she has never seen (292). To this point the plot is somewhat reminiscent of Jewett's "Martha's Lady" (1897).

The dénouement constitutes a resounding repudiation of this woman-centered world, however. In a bizarre twist, which is nevertheless congruent with the symbolic import of the story, we learn that Mrs. Meriden is the girl's long-lost mother. (Dream never learns this, however.) Then we find Dream rejecting this association for a male suitor. "After all what was a woman when it came to a man?" (299). "The world of women and the loves of women looked to her suddenly small and pale. She rebounded to the natural laws, and man the master came to his throne" (300).

Such a statement, written in 1910, would have been utterly repugnant, if not incomprehensible, to the earlier local colorists, and perhaps indeed to the earlier feminist Phelps. But it does show clearly how attitudes in the early twentieth century had changed, and how Phelps herself had moved to a position that indeed went so far as to assert male supremacy, relegating the "loves of women" to the status of "unnatural," and—perhaps the most startling reversal of the Victorian code—denying the mother bond. Mary E. Wilkins Freeman gives further evidence of the fragility of these bonds at the turn of the century.

The younger Phelps did, however, include many innovative portraits of unusual women, and did put forth a series of strong feminist position papers. Because these works extended the range of women's realism, I would like to treat them and her works of social criticism further, before concluding this chapter.

One of Phelps's earliest stories, "Margaret Bronson" (*Harper's* September 1865), presents one of the strongest female characters yet seen in American literature. Margaret is a southern woman "who carried pistols, had no desire to marry, and was not afraid of guerrillas." (The story is set during the Civil War.) Considered "strong-minded" by her neighbors, she runs the family plantation after her father's death, and frees the slaves. She also supports the Union during the war. Neighbors comment: "It would be a violation of nature for her to be a wife. *She* must be the man, and she'd rule everything with a rod of iron. To yield one inch of her own will would be torture to her." The plot is that one of her servants tips her off that her suitor's Union outfit is about to be attacked. She puts on her revolver and cloak and crosses the fields at night to warn them. Then she fights at his side and, when he's wounded, saves him by killing a rebel straggler.

"A Woman's Pulpit" (*Atlantic Monthly* July 1870, *Sealed Orders* 1879) presents another innovative woman character who becomes a minister in a rural New England town. The plot deals with the prejudices and other difficulties she encounters. Two of Phelps's late stories, too, present strong women characters. They are "The Autobiography of Aureola" (*Century* May 1904, *The Oath of Allegiance* 1909), which is about a town philanthropist, and "The Chief Operator" (*Harper's* July 1909, *The Oath of Allegiance*), a telephone operator who sacrifices her own life to save dozens of others in a flood. Nevertheless, these two stories are not so convincing as the early works.

Phelps's commitment to new roles and new rights for women was articulated in a series of articles published in the *Independent* in the early 1870s. In these she repeated the by-then classic feminist positions first developed by Mary Wollstonecraft nearly a century earlier. She lamented women's financial dependence on men, ridiculed women's concern with frivolous dress, said that women should be allowed access to higher education and to professional careers. She also, of course, supported the right to suffrage.

Her most significant article, "The True Woman" (*Independent* 12 October 1871), blasted this "scarecrow" image as one "patched up by men, and by those women who have no sense of character but such as they reflect from men." The "true woman" was perhaps the dominant cultural model for female behavior in the nineteenth century. It posited a retiring, self-effacing life-style, to revolve around the home and church (see chapter 2). Phelps argued that such a notion was no more accurate a description of "true" female character than "duplicity and dishonesty [were to] the negro character." Relations between the sexes should be characterized by "equalized independence of each other's control." Phelps asserted, perceptively, that we would only know woman's true nature "when she is free."

The Silent Partner (1871) and *Dr. Zay* are perhaps the most powerful of Phelps's works about this new type, the independent career woman. *Dr. Zay,* as noted above, recounts the life of a country physician. It is told, however, from the point of view of her suitor, which adds a note of irony that Sarah Orne Jewett eliminated in her treatment of the same subject, *A Country Doctor* (1884). Jewett's remains a stronger work; nevertheless, Phelps does draw some interesting contrasts between the suitor, Waldo Yorke, and the doctor, in this study of role reversal.

Yorke has been injured in an accident, which has reduced him to the status of a woman. "He lay there like a woman, reduced from activity to endurance" (119). At one point Dr. Zay rushes to rescue a drowning man, while he faints. She is always on the go, thinks in scientific terms, and is completely unflappable. "She went; he stayed. He suffered; she acted. He remembered; she forgot" (151). When he finally tells her that he loves her, she says, ". . . you are not in love . . . you are only nervous" (191). "How," he wonders, "was a man going to approach this new and confusing type of woman?" (186). Finally, however, she succumbs—a dénouement Jewett avoids—agreeing to try a new kind of marriage with "a new type of man" (244). They ride off, symbolically exchanging the reins from time to time, but we never learn how their marriage works out. When Phelps got into the nitty-gritty of marital relations she was considerably less sanguine.

The Silent Partner combines several of Phelps's early concerns. Like *Hedged In* it relates the cross-class support of one woman, Perley Kelso, a privileged daughter of a manufacturer, for a factory woman, Sip Garth. It describes in Dickensian detail the evils of factory life. And it is also a feminist novel; it focuses on the fact that Perley herself is discriminated against as a woman. Yet she decides to remain single and to pursue her vocation.

After her father dies, Perley is not allowed to accede to a partnership in the firm because of her sex. Instead she must remain "a silent partner," which means that her money remains invested but that the other (male) partners make all the decisions. They suggest she exert a "woman's influence" over her future husband, who is a partner. Perley had hoped that as a full partner she could change some of the dreadful conditions at the mill. Instead she becomes a kind of unofficial charity worker among the poor in the factory town.

Her career plots a descent into hell; in the opening chapter she is portrayed going to an opera in Boston wrapped in ermine, by the end she has been exposed to a series of horrifying examples of poverty and human degradation. The class distinction between her and the others is, once again, maintained by the workers' use of dialect and her use of standard English. Yet her identification is not with her male class peers but with the oppressed, especially the women.

Sip's story is fairly typical. Perley learns that Sip's father has recently died, but is unmourned because he had beaten Sip and her sister, Catty, a deformed fifteen-year-old deaf-mute, already headed toward alcoholism and prostitution. The father had continually stolen what food money they had for liquor. The others in the family have died "of drink and abuse."[11] Perley hears further stories from those who live in the factory slum. Phelps informs us that these are true and "may be found in the reports of the Massachusetts Bureau of Labor" (111).

Perley eventually rejects the proposals of suitors, who are her firm partners. "Possible wifedom was no longer an alluring dream" (261). She has seen too much, she feels her life's work lies in helping the poor. The prospect fills her with a sense of purpose.

Phelps wrote several other stories that dealt with social injustice. One of the earliest and one that helped to make her reputation was a lurid fictionalized account of the Pemberton mill fire that had actually occurred in Lawrence, Massachusetts, in 1860: "The Tenth of January" (*Atlantic Monthly* March 1868, *Men, Women and Ghosts*). While the gist of the story is a sentimental elaboration of a woman's failed love affair (despite antisentimental disclaimers: "I am not writing a novel. . . . Asenath was no heroine"), it does include a mild critique of the mill owners, whose irresponsibility and concern for profit led to acceptance of a structurally defective building and to the loss of scores of lives.

"The Madonna of the Tubs" (*Harper's* December 1885, *Fourteen to*

One) also depicts poverty, but, as the title indicates, is highly sentimental. A late story, "Unemployed" (*Harper's* November 1906, *The Oath of Allegiance*), somewhat realistically depicts the experience of unemployment. And another interesting late piece indicts the tactics of the Ku Klux Klan: "Fourteen to One" (*Fourteen to One*). The culmination of Phelps's novels of social activism was *A Singular Life* (1894), which concerns the saintly commitment of Emmanuel Bayard, a slum minister, to the temperance cause. Phelps once said, "Bayard is my dearest hero" (*Chapters,* 273). But *The Silent Partner* and *Hedged In* remain Phelps's most powerful works of social protest. Phelps never presented a systematic set of political remedies for social injustice, however (with the exception of her feminist essays). Rather, her vision of social melioration remained in the context of the social gospel.

Beyond the Gates (1883), shows Phelps's vision of the afterlife. The novel expresses a Swedenborgian notion of how people may change and grow toward perfection, that this perfect state may be sustained. Emmanuel Swedenborg (1688–1772) was a Swedish theologian whose ideas had gained considerable popularity in nineteenth-century America. His conception of the afterlife included the idea, seen in Phelps's works, that spirits live in cities similar to those on earth and engage in similar kinds of social intercourse.

Beyond the Gates espouses a doctrine of souls moved by love that is similar to Swedenborg's. In Phelps's vision a hierarchy of beings is ranged according to their degree of spiritual development or "personal holiness."[12] Those closest to earth are condemned to fruitless tasks; because they were too materialistic on earth, they lack the spiritual momentum to move beyond it to the purer reaches of heaven. Those who have learned to love on earth accede to a higher level, for the fundamental energy in this cosmos is love, the ultimate expression of which is divine love. Those who are in a state of higher love are radiant beings; the others are paler. Needless to say, those who were famous on earth and consumed by personal ambition (mostly men) are condemned to the lowest ranks, and those who loved quietly and humbly on earth (mostly women) accede to the higher realms. So heaven is a life of spiritual growth in cities similar to those on earth but without dirt, evil, sickness, fear, poverty, or death. In *The Gates Between* (1886) Phelps presents an example of how a soul is regenerated through this process. An ambitious male physician, for whom earthly success had been a kind of religion, is kept in a purgatorial state until he learns how to be a sensitive, caring, humble person. After this, he has a joyous reunion with his wife; he has effectively been resocialized for marriage. The later Phelps's vision of Utopia—enunciated in the 1880s—differs significantly, therefore, from that seen in works of the other local colorists. It is not of a rural world where strong women rule and where a women's culture flourishes. Rather it is a place devoted to the reform of negative male behavior. This is an important shift in emphasis.

Male–female relationships had always been one of Phelps's greatest fictional concerns. Some of her most perceptive works fall into this category. Generally speaking, the earlier works—that is, those before the late 1880s—present relationships in which women are stronger than men. Men are more often the invalids (literally and figuratively). Occasionally the male character is seen as the villain, or the system of roles is held responsible for the unhappiness of the female character. Several works, however, simply recount both partners' realization of how much they appreciate each other. Those after the 1880s include some, like *The Gates Between,* that call for the reform of the man; others call for the repentence of the woman. In later stories women are more often invalids and are more often seen negatively. This pattern conforms to the "fall from paradise" movement that characterizes Phelps's thematic development.

Phelps treated the theme of insensitive or brutal husbands or suitors in several stories; it culminated in her still-popular novel, *The Story of Avis* (1877). "Adam Gorrow" (*Harper's* January 1867), "Both Sides" (*Harper's* May 1869), and "Jack the Fisherman" (*Century* June 1887, *Fourteen to One* 1891) concern this theme. The men in "Adam Gorrow" and "Both Sides" are overly educated (Adam espouses Calvinist ideas); the women express a simple, rural outlook, which the author obviously favors. In this Phelps is consistent with the other local colorists. Jack, the fisherman, is an alcoholic who kills his wife in a drunken stupor; the story expresses an obvious feminist and temperance theme.

"No News" (*Atlantic Monthly* September 1868, *Men, Women and Ghosts* 1869) adumbrates the anti-marriage theme of *The Story of Avis,* which Kate Chopin was to use in her feminist classic, *The Awakening* (1899). The story concerns a woman's growing awareness of the stultifying effects of marriage. It is narrated by an elderly spinster who has a dim view herself of marriage: "The readiness with which young girls

will flit out of a tried, proved, happy home into the sole care and keeping of a man whom they have known three months . . . I do not pro-
fess to understand." Harrie Bird, the wife, gradually begins to feel herself cut off and alienated by her marriage. "She was growing out of the
world . . . turning into a fungus; petrifying; had forgotten whether
you called your seats at the Music Hall pews or settees." The arrival of
a sophisticated female visitor further aggravates the situation. Harrie
does not know, for example, that Tennessee had rejoined the Union
and Paulina, the visitor, does. Naturally the husband is attracted to
Paulina, and they begin a flirtation. The situation is resolved in typical
Phelps fashion when Harrie nearly dies in a boating incident that
brings the couple back together.

The Story of Avis carries the theme of "No News" much farther. It is
one of the roundest condemnations of the conventional role expecta-
tions in marriage yet presented. Avis, a young painter, is courted un-
successfully by Philip Ostrander. She has a strong resistance to marriage, wants to pursue a career as an artist, and declares, "I will never
yield, like other women!"[13] The narrator comments acidly: "God . . .
was not in a merciful [mood], when, knowing that they were to be in
the same world with men, he made women" (126).

However, Ostrander comes home a wreck from the Civil War, which
makes him more appealing in the curious power dynamics that characterize Phelps's relationships. He also promises that theirs will be a non-
traditional marriage. She succumbs, but soon learns the fraudulence of
this promise when he begins complaining about breakfast. She gradually becomes more and more despondent. "Sometimes, sitting bur-
dened with the child in her arms, she looked . . . off . . . with a stran-
gling desolation" (284). After her husband's flirtation with another
woman, and after he loses his job, they drift farther apart. He eventually leaves the area, and dies. But, even when released from the bonds
of marriage, Avis finds she can no longer paint. Her talent has been
wasted.

Another story, somewhat in the vein of Rose Terry Cooke, implicitly
criticizes the self-sacrifice of a dutiful wife who is left with no money
when her husband dies and who ends up in the poorhouse. This is "The
Relic of the Reverend Eliakim Twig" (*Independent* 29 December 1881,
changed to "His Relic" in *Fourteen to One*).

A number of Phelps's stories blame neither partner for the marital troubles but rely on the pattern of a near-disaster that leads to a renewed mutual appreciation of one another. "In the Gray Goth" (*Atlantic Monthly* November 1867) is typical of these: a married couple quarrels just before the husband is about to leave on a logging trip in midwinter. One of Phelps's great sensitivities is to the nuances of communication within a relationship, and this skill is evident even in this early story, where the details of the quarrel are presented convincingly. (She had neglected to cut the wick of the lamp correctly, and when he came home from his chores he found the house smoky, which he hated. He claimed that the fact that she neglected something he cared so much about on his last night home proved she did not love him. She said he did not deserve to be cared for, speaking like that, when she worked so hard. Etc.) On the trip he is lost for three days in a snowstorm. She joins the rescue party, which eventually finds him. Each repents the quarrel and vows to work harder at making things work. Similar stories include "Running the Risk" (*Independent* 28 June 1877, *Sealed Orders*), "The True Story of Guenever" (*Sealed Orders*), "The Madonna of the Tubs," and "Covered Embers" (*Harper's* August 1905, *The Oath of Allegiance*). "Fée" (*Century* March 1901, *The Empty House*), "The Romance of the Bill" (*Harper's Bazar* December 1902, *The Empty House*), and "A Sacrament" (*Harper's* December 1905, *The Oath of Allegiance*) all concern couples' happy reunions.

Some works, such as *The Gates Between*, require the repentence of the male. These include *Avery* (1902), "His Soul to Keep" (*Harper's* September 1908, *The Oath of Allegiance*), and *Though Life Do Us Part* (1908). In all these the man is a powerful politician or physician—a member of the patriarchal establishment. Some, however, require the reform of the woman or present fundamentally negative images of the women characters. These include "Saint Caligula" (*Independent* 5 December 1878, *Sealed Orders*) and three of Phelps's last works: *Walled In* (1907), "The Presence" (*Harper's Bazar* June 1910, *The Empty House*), and "The Empty House" (*Women's Home Companion* March–April 1910, *The Empty House*).

The fact that after *An Old Maid's Paradise* (1879) there are no happy single women in Phelps's work, nor any who form communities with other women, shows how Phelps's vision came to diverge radically from that of the other local colorists. Phelps seemed irresistably drawn toward marriage, despite her obvious ambivalence toward it. By the early years of the twentieth century she felt compelled to write her critique of the institution, *Confessions of a Wife* (1902), under a pseudonym. Phelps herself had married in 1888; by all accounts it was not a happy union. One could hypothesize that her late stories about happy marital reunions were a form of wish fulfillment.

Phelps, therefore, carried the traditions of local color literature into the twentieth century. Her late capitulation to conventional notions of male dominion and female submission show that by then women had "fallen" out of the woman-identified Eden of the Victorian era. While not of their caliber Phelps's transition helps to explain the cultural and moral atmosphere in which the next generation of women writers—Wharton, Cather, Glasgow, and Austin—began their careers. For this reason her place in the evolution of women's realism should not be neglected. But it is finally in the works of Sarah Orne Jewett and Mary E. Wilkins Freeman that the local color school culminated. It is they who produced its masterpieces.

7

Sarah Orne Jewett and the World of the Mothers

Sarah Orne Jewett incorporated the perceptions of women's literary realism developed by her predecessors in the local color school to produce an authentically female-identified vision of her own that moved beyond their limits. Hers is a woman's vision of transcendence, but it is no longer one of naive optimism as seen in Stowe or in the early Phelps. There is in Jewett a recognition of the troubles that concern the late Phelps and Freeman—anxiety over an encroaching male dominion, the "burglars in paradise." With Jewett, neither the anxieties nor the burglars prevail. The encroachment is resisted, the female sanctuary preserved.

But Cooke's intuition that evil and alienation may exist even in this country setting is incorporated in Jewett's final synthesis. Jewett adds to the gallery of strong and authentic female characters developed by the local colorists. But their optimistic doctrine of salvation by works is tempered in the late Jewett by a growing sense of the fragility of any human endeavor. We have seen where Elizabeth Stuart Phelps's hopes for women's fulfillment were blocked in the 1880s. Jewett was able to transcend this impasse by establishing a vision of a supportive community of women, sustained by a kind of matriarchal Christianity, and by traditions of women's lore and culture.[1]

Yet Jewett's was not an escapist Utopia. She did not leave stubborn and painful realities behind. It is indeed the tension between the "fallen," alienated world of real experience and the transcending vision of a supportive, fulfilling community that gives power to her greatest work. The sense of elegy which so many have remarked in Jewett's work is a lamentation for the tentative nature of human accomplishment—and especially for the artificially limited possibilities of emotional and intellectual development afforded women—but at the same time there is a celebration of the transfiguring moments in which the human community—again sustained primarily by women—coheres.

In order to understand Jewett's accomplishment it is necessary to review her theory of literature, a theory whose originality has not been sufficiently appreciated. For it was this theory that enabled her to reach beyond her predecessors and to create an imaginative realm that passes beyond the historical limitations to women's condition and prevails as an intuition of being. Jewett's literary doctrine may be derived from a series of statements she made at diverse times. Her father evidently gave her her earliest critical precepts, for she quoted his maxims often. One of these—that the writer should "tell things *just as they are*"[2]—is a straightforward articulation of realist theory, and a piece of advice Jewett conscientiously followed. The second important parental counsel was inscribed in the young artist's 1871 diary:

Father said this one day "A story should be managed so that it should *suggest* interesting things to the *reader* instead of the author's doing all the thinking for him, and setting it before him in black and white. The best compliment is for the reader to say 'Why didn't he put in "this" or "that" ' "[3]

The implications of this statement lead far from realist doctrine; indeed point strongly in the direction of symbolism, especially as it developed in France in the late nineteenth century. One of Jewett's acknowledged masters, Flaubert, is himself an example of a writer who hovered on the edge between realism and symbolism, a tendency also marked in his American disciple. Jewett noted that she had tacked two mottos from Flaubert up on her secretary so that she could see them whenever she began to write. These were: "Ecrire la vie ordinaire comme on écrit l'histoire" and "Ce n'est pas de faire rire, ni de faire pleurer, ni de vous mettre à fureur, mais d'agir à la façon de la nature, c'est à dire de faire rêver." Curiously, the first statement—that one should write about ordinary life as if one were writing history—is a fairly direct piece of realist theory. The second, however—that the writer's job is to "faire rêver," to make one dream—is more difficult to specify, but nevertheless brings to mind the Symbolists, who perceived the artist's task in similar terms. The writer must evoke, suggest, hint at the existence of a higher realm, a transcendent realm, by means of earthly objects, characters, and relationships.

Emmanuel Swedenborg's doctrine of correspondences—that there is a correlation between the microcosm and the macrocosm, between this realm "here below" and that realm beyond—was one which the Symbolists absorbed in their theory. As we have seen, some of Swedenborg's ideas, including a version of the correspondences doctrine, were used by Elizabeth Stuart Phelps in the *Gates* series. Jewett was also a student of Swedenborg's theosophy. She once wrote that she found "a sense of it under everything else."[4] Jewett, however, never resorted to the didactic interpretation of Swedenborg found in Phelps's works. Rather, like the late Symbolists she preferred the effect of the unstated resonance, a suggestion of things beyond, a hint at transcending powers; but she never stated the existence of such realities, nor attempted to depict them in her fiction. She was not really interested in a literal heaven, but rather in the hints of such a reality that we intuit within this world. She once noted that she found "something transfiguring in the best of friendship" (*Letters,* Fields, ed., 126). Her real concern was with the glimpses of transcendence that occur in this life, and between people. She remained a humanist.

Jewett once avowed an interest in writing moral allegory, especially of the kind Tolstoy used in some of his stories. She noted that she too had tried for this effect in several of her stories, notably "Lady Ferry," "Beyond the Toll-Gate," and "The Gray Man."[5]

"Lady Ferry" (*Old Friends and New* 1879) is a story rejected for the *Atlantic Monthly* by Howells, undoubtedly for its lack of realism. It is a supernatural tale about a woman allegedly condemned to immortality. Mysterious nocturnal happenings occur in her home the night the young narrator visits. Later, as an adult the visitor returns to find Lady Ferry's grave. The story is not fully successful, but it does have those hints of another dimension that Jewett was to use more effectively in later works.

"Beyond the Toll-Gate" (*Sunday Afternoon* March 1878, *Play Days* 1878) is a juvenile story about a young girl who ventures beyond her yard, through a toll-gate where she meets two elderly women who treat her as a special guest. The message of this moral allegory is that, while "it costs something to go through," often there are surprising riches on the other side of the gate. It is an optimistic moral of salvation by works and by exertion of one's free will, consistent with young Jewett's philosophy.

"The Gray Man" (*A White Heron* 1886) is about a mysterious unsmiling stranger who comes to town, an allegorical figuration of Death. Another story, "A Christmas Guest" (*Wide Awake* January 1887, *Uncollected Stories* 1971), is also an allegory about a stranger who has a revitalizing effect on family members one Christmas Eve; he seems to be a Christ-figure. Early in her career Jewett had acknowledged a desire to include a level of "silent scripture," of moral meaning, in her work.[6] This she did—obviously in her early works, more subtly in the later ones.

Jewett expressed on several occasions an interest in what might be called spiritualism, as had on a more superficial level Harriet Beecher Stowe and Elizabeth Stuart Phelps. Stowe was interested in communicating with the dead through séances, Ouija boards, and planchettes, and included spiritualistic episodes in some of her works of fiction. Phelps wrote a rather effective story about spirit rappings, "The Day of My Death" (*Harper's* October 1868, *Men, Women and Ghosts* 1869), but in her autobiography denied being a spiritualist.[7] Jewett, however, was less interested in such spectacular manifestations of spiritual reality as séances and more interested in meditations on questions such as whether death was a moment of awakening. Will we, in an afterlife celebrate our deathday as we do our birthday here? (*Letters*, Fields, ed., 16, 29). She speculated that in that perfect realm a writer's thoughts might bloom untended without "the business part," which she found "noxious." But she reflected, ". . . being in this world everything must have a body, and a material part, so covers and leaves and publishing generally come under that head, and is another thing to make us wish to fly away and be at rest!" (*Letters*, Fields, ed., 62–63). Perhaps her most intriguing speculation about the spiritual aspect of literature came at the death of her friend, poet Celia Thaxter. She remarked how she seemed to be able to see Celia's face and wondered, ". . . where imagination stops and consciousness of the unseen begins, who can settle that even to one's self?" (*Letters*, Fields, ed., 111–12).

Jewett's theory of art, therefore, must be seen in the context of her ruminations on spiritual reality, some of which had been inspired by Swedenborg. In a letter of counsel to a young writer Jewett coined the term "imaginative realism" to specify her ideal of great literature.[8] The term seems an appropriate one for her own literary theory; it implies that the writer deals not just with the "facts" of the story but rather uses those facts to point to a dimension beyond the real. This may be a moral level, as seen in her early stories; it may be the level of the supernatural. Or, it may be an imaginative level that echoes beyond the bare facts of the story. Her father's injunction that the writer suggest ideas that gestate in the reader's own mind is what Jewett meant by "imaginative realism." One must allow for the kind of experience that Jewett herself had at Celia Thaxter's death, that flickering connection between the imagination and "the unseen."

Jewett once complained about Jane Austen's realism: ". . . all the reasoning is done for you and all the thinking. . . . It seems to me like hearing somebody talk on and on and on, while you have no part in the conversation, and merely listen."[9] Again, the idea is that too much realism can block the flights of imagination Jewett wishes art to precipitate.

In complimenting her friend Sarah Wyman Whitman for her interpretation of "Martha's Lady" (1897), Jewett wrote, "You bring something to the reading of a story that the story would go very lame without." And: "It is," she asserted, "those unwritable things that the story holds in its heart, if it has any, that make the true soul of it, and these must be understood, and yet how many a story goes lame for lack of that understanding" (*Letters,* Fields, ed., 112). This then is the meaning of the term "imaginative realism"; it is writing that stirs one's imagination, that makes one dream. And it is this kind of writing that Jewett bequeathed to her protégée, Willa Cather.

Two fundamental themes, both of which we have traced in earlier local colorists, run through Jewett's work. One is the tension between the conflicting attractions of rural and urban life. And the other is the tension between individualism and the participation of the self in a community identity. The former is seen positively in a series of spinsters who prefer to live alone, but is regarded as destructive by Jewett when it is carried to an extreme. The importance of a transcending community is stressed in the late works. It is a community primarily of women and sustained by a kind of matriarchal Christianity and by other traditions of women's lore. It is in these later works—after the mid-1880s—that Jewett's own imaginative realism finds its greatest expression.

The tension between country and city runs throughout Jewett's work. Jewett's own love of the country is evidenced in scores of comments she made in letters and in the loving detail she used to describe its realities in literally hundreds of stories. Already in *Deephaven* (1877), her earliest collection, one senses, however, a decided ambivalence toward rural life. On the one hand, it is a place where strong, authentic women flourish, such as Mrs. Bonny, who lives in an isolated cabin deep in the woods, wears men's clothing, smokes tobacco, and has an extensive knowledge of herbs and wild life. "She [has] an amazing store of tradition and superstition,"[10] and is uncontaminated by civilization (she anticipates Jewett's great matriarch, Almira Todd, of *The Country of the Pointed Firs* [1896]).

The rural world also encourages the development of one's psychic powers and one's sensitivity to spiritual realities. One of the sketches in *Deephaven,* "Cunner-Fishing," particularly explores this issue. The two young summer visitors remark how close to nature country people are and how this leads them to appreciate "the mysterious creative power which is at work with them on their familiar farms." Further: "They believe in dreams, and they have a kind of fetichism, and believe so heartily in supernatural causes" (130). Kate, one of the girls, observes, ". . . the more one lives out of doors the more personality there seems to be in what we call inanimate things" (131). Captain Sands, who had told the girls of a psychic episode, believes that people's psychic faculties are only embryonic in this stage of their development, comparing these to the legs of "polliwogs" (tadpoles)—useless until the creatures turn into frogs. Similarly, people's psychic "fac'lties" remain unused, but shall be turned "to account some time or 'nother" (124). The rural world, therefore, is the place closest to the "beyond" in Jewett's thinking, and the place where spiritual realities are most likely to be sensed. This idea is central in Jewett's later works.

On the other hand, Jewett, like Rose Terry Cooke, knew that rural life had its drawbacks. *Deephaven* includes stark images of poverty, deprivation, and even wife abuse. Other stories reveal an awareness of the boredom, isolation, and spiritual poverty that remote reaches can engender. In "A Bit of Shore Life" (*Atlantic Monthly* August 1879, *Old Friends and New*) Jewett describes the "cheerless" and "morbid" lives of elderly women:

They are very forlorn; they dwell persistently upon any troubles which they have; and their petty disputes with each other have a tragic hold upon their thoughts, sometimes being handed down from one generation to the next. Is it because their world is so small, and life affords so little amusement and pleasure, and is at best such a dreary round of the dullest housekeeping? (244).

Here Jewett approaches the vision of rural life seen in the works of Mary E. Wilkins Freeman or indeed Edith Wharton.

Like her local color predecessors Jewett often presents a narrator persona who comes into the rural area as a visitor, who speaks standard English, while the natives speak in dialect. She is able to escape from the smallness and the boredom of country life by returning to the city, though often she finds herself spiritually rejuvenated by the visit. This is indeed the pattern of *The Country of the Pointed Firs*. Yet Jewett does not consistently take the part of the "summer visitor." In her late, great story, "Martha's Lady," she claimed to identify with a humble, nearly illiterate servant girl, who falls in love with a sophisticated urban woman. "Nobody must say that Martha was dull," Jewett commented, "it is only I" (*Letters*, Fields, ed., 113).

In *The Country of the Pointed Firs*, however, where the rural world assumes the dimensions of a spiritual landscape, the "outsider" status of the narrator takes on greater meaning than in earlier local color works. For, it implies a degree of alienation from the fullness of communal and spiritual being that the area has come to symbolize. Perhaps ultimately it is a comment on the growing sense of distance the American woman felt from the matriarchal, female-identified realm described in *Pointed Firs*.

The second central theme in Jewett's work is that of individualism versus community. At least a dozen of Jewett's early stories, that is, up until the mid-1880s, describe strong independent single women who win their way by exerting their will, taking charge of events. In other words, they take care of themselves through their own works. These include "A Lost Lover" (*Atlantic Monthly* March 1878, *Old Friends and New*), "A Late Supper" (*Sunday Afternoon* January 1878, *Old Friends and New*), "A Bit of Shore Life," " Miss Becky's Pilgrimage" (*Independent* 1 September 1881, *Country By-Ways* 1881), "A Guest at Home" (*Congregationalist* 29 November 1882, *Uncollected Stories*), "A New Parishioner" (*Atlantic Monthly* April 1883, *The Mate of the Daylight* 1884), and "Farmer Finch" (*Harper's* January 1885, *A White Heron*).

Jewett's feminist novel about the young woman who decides to become a physician, *A Country Doctor* (1884), also depicts an independent woman who rejects a suitor in order to pursue her career. Questions about the loneliness or insufficiency of a solitary life, such as plagued Phelps, are not raised by Jewett. Nan Prince is dedicated to her career and that is sufficient. In a later, juvenile novel, *Betty Leicester* (1890), Jewett emphasizes that young girls ought not to wait for romance to sweep them away but rather ought to develop a sense of self-reliance and not depend on others to make their way for them.

After the mid-1880s, however, Jewett began to stress the importance not so much of self-reliance but of orientation toward a community that provides emotional support and moral encouragement. These communities were occasionally just of two, but Jewett was not obsessed with marriage like Phelps. One early story, "Miss Sydney's Flowers" (*Independent* 16 July 1874, *Old Friends and New*), deals with the opening up of a stiff, solitary spinster to a relationship with others, and to feelings of compassion. But it is really only in the late 1880s that the majority of the stories with this theme appear.

Several of them deal with feuds being mended, such as "A Visit Next Door" (*Congregationalist* 10 January 1884, *Uncollected Stories*), "Law Lane" (*Scribner's* December 1887, *The King of Folly Island* 1888), "Fair Day" (*Scribner's* August 1888, *Strangers and Wayfarers* 1890), and "Bold Words at the Bridge" (*McClure's* April 1899, *Uncollected Stories*). Some deal with spinsters whose loneliness is acknowledged, and some with those whose isolation is ended when they are united with loved ones or whose lives are integrated with others. The former include "Miss Peck's Promotion" (*Scribner's* June 1887, *The King of Folly Island*), "A Village Shop" (*The King of Folly Island*), "The Growtown 'Bugle'" (*Harper's Weekly* 18 August 1888, *Uncollected Stories*), and "Going to Shrewsbury" (*Atlantic Monthly* July 1889, *Strangers and Wayfarers*). The latter include "A Garden Story" (*Independent* 22 July 1886, *Uncollected Stories*), "The Town Poor" (*Atlantic Monthly* July 1890, *Strangers and Wayfarers*), "Aunt Cynthy Dallett" (originally published as "The New-Year Guests," *Harper's Bazar* 11 January 1896, *The Queen's Twin* 1899), "Martha's Lady" (*Atlantic Monthly* October 1897, *The Queen's Twin*), and "Sister Peacham's Turn" (*Harper's* November 1902, *Uncollected Stories*).

There are also several minor stories that concern the union or reunion of men and women in marriage. These include "Told in the Tavern" (*New York World* 15 April 1894, *Uncollected Stories*), "A Native of Winby" (*Atlantic Monthly* May 1891, *A Native of Winby* 1893), "A Winter Courtship" (*Atlantic Monthly* February 1889, *Strangers and Wayfarers*), "A Second Spring" (*Harper's* December 1893, *The Life of Nancy* 1895), "All My Sad Captains" (*Century* September 1895, *The Life of Nancy*), "A Change of Heart" (*Ladies' Home Journal* April 1896, *Uncollected Stories*), "A Pinch of Salt" (*Boston Evening Transcript* 30 October 1897, *Uncollected Stories*), and "A Spring Sunday" (*McClure's* May 1904, *Uncollected Stories*), Jewett's last published story.

"The Flight of Betsey Lane" (*Scribner's* August 1893, *A Native of Winby*) is a story that provides a synthesis of the conflicting needs of self-assertion on the one hand and community participation on the other. The central character is a resident of the Byfleet Poor-house, a community of elderly women. After receiving an unexpected gift of money, Betsey disappears one day. The other members fear she is lost. But Betsey had merely decided to assert her independence by attending the Centennial celebration in Philadelphia. After her adventurous fling Betsey returns home to spend her final years within her community of friends.

It was in the late 1880s—beginning probably with "A White Heron" in 1886—that many of Jewett's greatest works began to appear. Their claim to greatness lies justly in her effective use of imaginative realism. For, in these works, while it is too much to claim allegorical meanings, figures and forces do come to represent something beyond themselves. The rural world so central to local color literature becomes in Jewett's handling a spiritual landscape, a metaphorical realm, where she expresses her vision of the human condition. "A White Heron," "Miss Tempy's Watchers," *The Country of the Pointed Firs*, and "The Foreigner" are perhaps the most significant of these late works, though several others also deserve attention.

"A White Heron" (*A White Heron* 1886) is one of the most important stories in this study, for, as noted in Chapter 2, it repudiates the Cinderella text so central to earlier women's literature and prepares the way for the creation of the matriarchal country of *Pointed Firs*. It is another story Howells rejected for the *Atlantic Monthly*. He thought it too romantic. It is not really a romance, however; if anything, it is an antiromance. It culminates the antiromance tradition we have seen as a hallmark of women's literary realism.

The facts of the story are these: a young country girl, Sylvia, lives with her grandmother in a pastoral rural setting. The girl had had an earlier life in a "crowded manufacturing town" where she had been harassed by a "great red-faced boy" (162–63).[11] One day an ornithologist comes to the area; he is seeking a white heron for his collection of stuffed birds. When the girl first hears the man she is "horror-stricken." It is "not a bird's whistle, which would have a sort of friendliness, but a boy's whistle, determined and somewhat aggressive." He is immediately perceived as "the enemy" (163).

During the man's stay with the girl and her grandmother, Sylvia gradually loosens her guard, although "she could not understand why he killed the very birds he seemed to like so much" (166). Nevertheless, a mild possibility of romance appears to sway Sylvia toward the stranger. We learn that "the woman's heart, asleep in the child, was vaguely thrilled by a dream of love" (166). When he asks her to tell him the white heron's location, she seriously considers doing so. This is partly because she wants to please him, partly perhaps because of his offer of cash (they are poor, but this does not seem to represent a serious consideration for the girl), and finally and most important is her own pride. She is proud of her knowledge of the woodlands and wants to show it off. "What fancied triumph and delight and glory for the later morning when she could make known the secret!" (167).

The story concludes after a nocturnal quest in which she climbs a tall tree and sees much that she had never seen before—the ocean nearby, ships at sea, as well as the white bird. In the end, however, she cannot tell the man the bird's location. "The murmur of the pine's green branches is in her ears, she remembers how the white heron came flying through the golden air and how they watched the sea and the morning together, and Sylvia cannot speak; she cannot tell the heron's secret and give its life away" (171). For this stand she loses the ornithologist's potential friendship and love.

The story holds a significance beyond these "facts," however. Seen in the context of the traditions of the women's realism of the local colorists, one may interpret the dynamics of the story as representing a clash between a patriarchal value system (that symbolized by the urban male with his gun—itself a symbol of Western industrial imperialism) and a female-centered peaceful world, the matriarchal Utopia first seen in Stowe and developed by Phelps until she acknowledged the encroachment of "burglars in paradise."

Jewett, nonetheless, even in this story acknowledges the limitations of this country arcadia. Indeed, the main appeal of the ornithologist is that he widens Sylvia's horizons, he sparks her interest and her curiosity. The narrator comments: "Alas, if the great wave of human interest which flooded for the first time this dull little life should sweep away the satisfactions of an existence heart to heart with nature and the dumb life of the forest!" (168).

In another story of this period, "Miss Peck's Promotion" (*Scribner's* June 1887, *The King of Folly Island*), Jewett similarly urged that the appeal of a potential suitor lay in the fact that "he stood . . . for a widened life . . . a larger circle of human interests; in fact, his existence had made all the difference between her limited rural home and that connection with the great world which even the most contracted parsonage is sure to hold" (189).

Miss Peck's minister and Sylvia's ornithologist represent wider horizons, growth, expanding knowledge to the women. And yet both prove to be treacherous. Miss Peck's minister rejects her after exploiting her labor, and Sylvia's friend would destroy her woodland sanctuary. On one level, therefore, "A White Heron" appears to express the profound ambivalence women of the late nineteenth century felt as they were beginning to move out of the female-centered world of the home into male-centered institutions such as universities. The appeal of knowledge is there, but the fear that such knowledge will destroy their female world and its values is also quite evident.

Sylvia's story is, as Annis Pratt points out, a reverse fairy tale.[12] Traditionally, it is the handsome prince who comes to save Cinderella or Sleeping Beauty from lives of mundane reality. Here we have the prince only initiating the "awakening." The most important growth, symbolized by the girl's nighttime journey, is done by the girl herself. It is this knowledge—*of her own world*—that strengthens her resolve to defend and protect her rural surroundings. It is because of her renewed identification with this female world that she is able to resist the male intruder (the "burglar") and his destructive ways. In contradistinction to the traditional fairy tale, or romance, she rejects the prince, in favor of a female world.

Significantly, in Grimm's version of the fairy tale, Cinderella plants a twig on her mother's grave out of which, "nourished by her tears of lamentation," grows a tree from which comes a "white bird that is her mother's spirit."[13] The white bird in "A White Heron" is a similar representation. Sylvia's rural sanctuary is the world of the mothers. Her stand is the stand of nineteenth-century womanhood guarding the female community but sensing that it may be a losing battle. Jewett is the last apologist for this matriarchal world.

"Miss Tempy's Watchers" (*Atlantic Monthly* March 1888, *The King of Folly Island*) is another story that has profound importance and touches upon realms of spiritual efficacity that go beyond natural, material causes. The story concerns the wake of Temperance Dent, a woman who had in life an almost psychic sensitivity to the feelings of others. "She always sensed things, and got just the p'int you meant" (241). She also seemed to have a magic or supranatural power to bring things to life. In the spring she was able to communicate a vitality into her old quince tree. "She'd go out in the spring and tend to it, and look at it so pleasant, and kind of expect the old thorny thing into bloomin'." And: "She was just the same with folks" (241).

Tempy had chosen two old schoolmates for the wake, Mrs. Crowe, a wealthy woman of some social position, and Sarah Ann Binson, a poor spinster who had the responsibility of supporting "an inefficient widowed sister and six unpromising and unwilling nieces and nephews." Tempy had evidently chosen these two deliberately, in "some hope that they might become closer friends in the period of intimate partnership, and that the richer woman might better understand the burdens of the poorer" (234). Her plan is a success. During the evening Mrs. Crowe begins to eulogize their lost friend, noting especially her generosity. She resolves to try to become more charitable herself. As time passes it becomes clear that even in death Tempy's spirit is able to "expect into blooming" feelings of sisterhood and community between the two women. As they begin to drowse, "Sister Binson closed her eyes first . . . and Mrs. Crowe glanced at her compassionately, with a new sympathy for the hard-worked little woman" (242).

In a study entitled *Communities of Women: An Idea in Fiction,* Nina Auerbach selects this story to exemplify the type. The women, brought together momentarily "at the margins of the social and natural world," achieve "an almost magical affinity with the sources of transformation and rebirth." A "miraculous sisterhood" has been formed.[14] "Miss Tempy's Watchers" furthers Jewett's vision of a rural sanctuary where the spiritual powers of transcendence are sustained by women, who are in touch with nature and with one another. It is becoming a realm of mystical female powers.

"The Courting of Sister Wisby," published the year before "Miss Tempy's Watchers" (*Atlantic Monthly* May 1887, *The King of Folly Island*), extends the development of the Jewett country matriarch, the natural herbologist, in the figure of Mrs. Goodsoe. It also refines a narrative device Jewett had used frequently and was to use again to greater significance in *The Country of the Pointed Firs:* that of the woman visitor encountering a native who tells her a local story. In "Sister Wisby" the relationship between the visitor and the native, Mrs. Goodsoe, takes on almost equal weight with the tale itself. In *Pointed Firs* that relationship dominates the work, perhaps suggesting an increasing desire by the urban visitor to reach and communicate with the rural women who have come to embody a mystical potency.

Mrs. Goodsoe is the bearer of a matrilineal tradition of herb medicine. She learned it from her mother. She scorns modern technological progress and particularly modern medicine. She castigates young doctors who are "bilin' over with book-larnin'" but who are "truly ignorant of what to do for the sick" (57).

Like her mother Mrs. Goodsoe is a purist. Herbs should be derived from the immediate environment and never imported. One suspects that she believes that people, too, are best left in their proper environments and not uprooted and removed to alien contexts. She is suspicious of modern rapid transportation. People need not travel all over. "In old times . . . they stood in their lot an' place, and weren't all just alike, either, same as pine-spills" (59). The visitor suggests that some modern inventions have broadened and enriched people's lives, but Mrs. Goodsoe disagrees. Again we sense an ambivalence between the values and traditions of the female rural world, as opposed to the benefits of "male" technological progress.

Several stories written during this period deal with tyrannies imposed within families, usually by patriarchal figures; they form a kind of counterpoint to which the images of community seen in other works seem a response. The most graphic and the most hopeless of these are depicted in "The King of Folly Island" (*Harper's* December 1886, *The King of Folly Island*) and "The Landscape Chamber" (*Atlantic Monthly* 1887, *The King of Folly Island*).

In the first story George Quint has exiled himself, his wife, and his daughter on an island and has established a virtual dictatorship over the women. "It was upon the women of the household that an unmistakeable burden of isolation had fallen" (25). In a dénouement reminiscent of Rose Terry Cooke, both women die; the one from a lack of affection and community and the other from consumption aggravated by a lack of care. In one episode the daughter, Phebe, is so eager to participate in communal affairs that she resorts to watching a funeral procession on a neighboring island through a spyglass.

In "The Landscape Chamber" a daughter is tyrannized by a Calvinistic patriarch, who has withdrawn from society and forbids her social intercourse. The narrator-visitor encourages the girl to resist: "Among human beings there is freedom. . . . We can climb to our best possibilities, and outgrow our worst inheritance" (114). But, despite this optimistic assertion of a salvation-by-works philosophy, the family appears doomed to some kind of preestablished fate.

In two stories, "Mère Pochette" (*Harper's* March 1888, *The King of Folly Island*) and "Dan's Wife" (*Harper's Bazar* 2 August 1889), the tyrant is a woman, but she relents and social harmony results. "A Neighbor's Landmark" (*Century* December 1894, *The Life of Nancy*) pits a tyrannical father against his wife and daughter. Once again the issue is the preservation of the natural world from industrial destruction. In this case the tyrant, John Packer, wants to sell two giant pines on his property to a greedy capitalist. The daughter and wife feel that the trees are almost animate beings, familiar parts of their lives. Finally they succeed in protecting the trees from destruction.

"In Dark New England Days" (*Century* October 1890, *Strangers and Wayfarers*) picks up the theme of women's resistance to tyranny and combines it with the idea of rural women having magical powers. In this case, however, the powers are of darkness; the women practice witchcraft.

Two sisters, Hannah and Betsey Knowles, have been tyrannized by their father for years, and at his death receive an inheritance: a chest of gold coins. Unfortunately, it is stolen, and the women, feeling bitterly cheated, vow to have vengeance on the suspected thief. They accuse a neighbor, Enoch Holt, of the crime. He is tried and acquitted. After the trial Hannah accuses him to his face, and when he raises his right hand to swear his innocence, she lays a curse upon it. As the years pass, three members of the Holt family, including Enoch, lose the use of their right hand. The sisters have resorted to witchcraft, to psychic vengeance, to express their anger over years of abuse and oppression and for their final, bitter disappointment

The Country of the Pointed Firs (1896), together with a late story, "The Foreigner" (*Atlantic Monthly* August 1900), which has the same characters, is the most extended enunciation of Jewett's final vision of a transcending matriarchal realm. In this analysis, as in my earlier studies, I am following the original 1896 edition of *Pointed Firs*, which does not include the later interpolated stories "A Dunnet Shepherdess," "The Queen's Twin," and "William's Wedding."[15]

The Country of the Pointed Firs complexly interweaves many of the themes and motifs we have been tracing through this book. Through Jewett's handling of them in *Pointed Firs*, we can learn to understand their deeper significance. The ambivalence of the narrator-visitor may be seen to represent the historical anxieties of this generation of women, their distance from the matriarchal world of their foremothers, and their longing to reconnect with it. The world of rural Maine, the land of the pointed firs, however, emerges as a place on the edge of historical time; it is an almost timeless female realm that stands as a counterreality to the encroaching male world of modern technology. And while the work is marked by a tone of elegy, a sense that the rural world is irretrievably passing as an historical entity, there is nevertheless a sense of joy and of faith that such a world must also remain as a timeless way of being. The themes of isolation and community are thus brought to culmination. The community is an enduring world sustained by Jewett's great matriarch, Mrs. Todd, and her mother, Mrs. Blackett.

The work opens when a middle-aged woman returns to Dunnet Landing late in June. She is a writer from a city, probably Boston or New York. She has apparently come to this remote area seeking a place to write, but one also senses that she is in search of spiritual regeneration. This is especially emphasized in a late, unfinished sequel, "William's Wedding" (*Atlantic Monthly* July 1910), in which the visitor returns once again, escaping from "the hurry of life in a large town," to find herself feeling "solid and definite again, instead of a poor, incoherent being."

The visitor secures a room with Mrs. Almira Todd, the town herbalist and community healer. Mrs. Todd practices rites that belong to ages past. At times, like Miss Tempy and the Knowles sisters, she seems to have supranatural powers; she practices beneficent witchcraft. "There were some strange and pungent odors that roused a dim sense and remembrance of something in the forgotten past. Some of these might once have belonged to sacred and mystic rites, and have had some occult knowledge handed with them down the centuries" (4). In the evenings the women have long conversations over one of Mrs. Todd's concoctions, spruce beer. A sense of intimacy develops between them. The visitor comes to realize that Mrs. Todd ministers not only to people's physical ills but also to their spiritual needs. "It seemed sometimes as if love and hate and jealousy and adverse winds at sea might also find their proper remedies among the curious wild-looking plants in Mrs. Todd's garden" (5).

The narrator's sense of distance from the Dunnet Landing community is accentuated, however, when she watches a funeral procession from afar. The procession looks "futile and helpless" as it proceeds along "the edge of the rocky shore" (18). The narrator feels suddenly alone and unsure of her own place in the world. She longs "for a companion and for news from the outer world, which had been, half unconsciously, forgotten." She says, too: "I had now made myself and my friends remember that I did not really belong to Dunnet Landing."

After the funeral the first of a number of local characters presents himself to her. Captain Littlepage, an aged sea captain whose brains, it is suspected, have become somewhat addled over the years, scorns the modern world, and tells the visitor a story about a voyage during which men had caught a glimpse of the afterlife. Before he begins, Jewett notes that they could hear "the noise of the water on a beach below. It sounded like the strange warning wave that gives notice of the turn of the tide." At the same time, nearer at hand " a late golden robin, with the most joyful and eager of voices, was singing close by in a thicket of wild roses" (30). These two images, the wave and the robin, seem to symbolize the two states that are in conflict in this work: the wave suggesting the passage of history; the robin, the ageless pastoral world that transcends historical time.

Littlepage's voyage, she relates, ended in shipwreck in Arctic waters. When rescued, he encountered a half-mad Scotsman who told him of a voyage he had taken to far reaches of the northland, where he found "a strange sort of country . . . beyond the ice, and strange folks living in it" (35). The "folks" were shades, "all blowing gray figures," "fog-shaped men" (37). It was a land between the living and the dead, a "waiting place."

Littlepage's "waiting place" is another image of a timeless place beyond historical time. Dunnet Landing seems itself to be hanging in such a limbo. Not long after, when the narrator and Mrs. Todd stand looking out to sea, a ray of sunlight illuminates an outer island. It seems like "a sudden revelation of the world beyond this which some believe to be so near. 'That's where mother lives,' said Mrs. Todd" (45). The association of Mrs. Blackett, Almira Todd's mother, with transcendence is not accidental, for she presents a model of the matriarch who sustains communal life.

The relationship between Mrs. Todd and the visitor, too, forms an experience of transcendence. And Jewett draws the connection between the afterworld described by Littlepage and the sanctuary created between the two women in Mrs. Todd's cottage: "I felt for a moment," the narrator remarks, "as if it were part of a spell and incantation, and as if my enchantress would now begin to look like the cobweb shapes of the arctic town" (47).

Mrs. Blackett lives out on an island with her son, William. Mrs. Todd and the narrator visit her out there and once again feel the magic of genuine hospitality. Later they all attend a family reunion "up country" which provides the climactic image of community in the work. Beforehand, however, we are introduced to Joanna, one of Jewett's extreme isolates, who seems to culminate the local color tradition of Calvinist oppression. Joanna's story, significantly, is narrated in the context of a reunited friendship. Mrs. Fosdick, a guest of Mrs. Todd, tells of Joanna one evening as the women are gathered around a Franklin stove. A northeaster rages outside.

Joanna had isolated herself on an island years before, partly out of unrequited love, but more out of a sense of Calvinistic self-flagellation for having committed the "unpardonable sin" of blaspheming God in the wake of her disappointment. Mrs. Todd recalls that she herself had in her youth voyaged out to the island with a minister to try to persuade Joanna to return. The minister tried a typically patriarchal "fire and brimstone" lecture to get her to relent, while Mrs. Todd tried a gentler approach. She gave Joanna a coral pin; but Joanna returned the pin and refused to leave her self-imposed isolation. Jewett suggests that Joanna symbolizes a spiritual state: "in the life of each of us . . . there is a place remote and islanded, and given to endless regret or secret happiness; we are each the uncompanioned hermit and recluse of an hour or a day" (132).

The climactic event of *Pointed Firs* is the Bowden family reunion, which all attend. The day is elevated to the level of religious significance: "Such a day as this has transfiguring powers. [It] gives to those who are dumb their chance to speak, and lends beauty to the plainest face" (156–57). It is a matriarchal happening. Mrs. Blackett rules supreme: "'Mother's always the queen,' said Mrs. Todd" (161). The old Bowden home looks like "a motherly brown hen waiting for the flock" (159). As Mrs. Blackett makes her way toward the reunion, people light up with delight to see her once again. "One revelation after another was made of the constant interest and intercourse that had linked the far island and these scattered farms into a golden chain of love and dependence" (147). The visitor-narrator feels a part of this ceremonial, as opposed to the funeral rite earlier. The experience is one of drawing into a timeless ritual, of drawing closer to a fuller participation in being. "The sky, the sea, have watched poor humanity at its rites so long; we were no more a New England family celebrating its own existence and simple progress; we carried the tokens and inheritance of all such households from which this had descended, and were only the latest of our line" (163).

Even this rite, however, is seen in the context of forces and powers that are much more powerful: the sea and the sky, which have watched "poor humanity" for so long. This world is doomed, not only by the powers of encroaching "progress," but also by the greater forces of death, mortality, and time passing.

Nevertheless, even in this awesome context, figures manage to renew their vitality and to claim a spiritual victory. The narrator notes the effect the affair has on Mrs. Todd: "I could see that sometimes when [she] had seemed limited and heavily domestic, she had simply grown sluggish for lack of proper surroundings" (173–74). "It was not the first time that I was full of wonder at the waste of human ability in this world, as a botanist wonders at the wastefulness of nature, the thousand seeds that die, the unused provision of every sort" (174).

The summer comes finally to an end. The visitor must leave. The parting scene between her and Mrs. Todd heightens the sense of elegy. Mrs. Todd tries to make it a parting without good-bys but the narrator notes, "I could not part so; I ran after her . . . but she shook her head and waved her hand without looking back . . ." (210). The visitor realizes that this phase of her life has ended. "So we die before our own eyes; so we see some chapters of our lives come to their natural end"

(210). As she leaves, she discovers that Mrs. Todd has bequeathed to her Joanna's coral pin. The brooch may be seen to symbolize the transitions in women's lives that we have noted in this book—from a period of patriarchal and Calvinistic oppression, to a matriarchal world seen in Mrs. Todd, and finally to the younger generation, unsure of whether it belongs to the women's world of Dunnet Landing or to the masculine world of the twentieth century. The fact that the narrator cannot stay in Dunnet Landing suggests the latter implication.

"The Foreigner" follows a narrative pattern similar to the episode in *Pointed Firs* in which Joanna's story is told. A "nor'easter" is beating outside the cottage while Mrs. Todd and the visitor sit near the fire within. Mrs. Todd recalls that Eliza Tolland had died on a similar night forty years previously.

Eliza had been brought to Dunnet Landing as a young bride by her husband, a sea captain who had met her in Jamaica. She spoke little English and was perceived as a "foreigner." Mrs. Blackett, however, had urged that Almira welcome the woman, exerting the same kind of hospitality as seen in *Pointed Firs*. It turns out that Mrs. Todd's efforts on behalf of Eliza pay off in ways she could not have foreseen. She learns much about herbs from Eliza, and discovers that the woman works "charms" in her home. After the captain is lost at sea, Eliza becomes more and more isolated.

Mrs. Todd stays with her the night of her death. Strange spiritualistic events occur. At one point Eliza sits bolt upright and reaches her arms toward the door. Mrs. Todd looks, and there is "a woman's dark face lookin' right at us . . . a pleasant enough face, shaped somethin' like Mis' Tolland's" (322–23). Eliza says it is her dead mother. "'You saw her, didn't you?' she said . . . an' I says, '*Yes, dear, I did; you ain't never goin' to feel strange an' lonesome no more.*' An' then in a few quiet moments 't was all over. I felt they'd gone way together." Mrs. Todd comments further, ". . . you know plain enough there's somethin' beyond this world" (323). Almira later learns that she is the beneficiary of Mrs. Tolland's will.

The story furthers Jewett's matriarchal vision. The spirit-figure is a woman, a mother. Transcendence and redemption are associated with her. The women help one another. Mrs. Todd and Mrs. Blackett have helped Eliza through her early isolation; her mother's spirit helps Eliza through the moment of death. The matrilineal connection is clear: Mrs.

Tolland bequeaths her wealth and her knowledge of herbs to another woman, Mrs. Todd. It is women who are in touch with the spiritual world and who seem to be able to inject into this world something of its magic and transcendence.

Sarah Orne Jewett created a symbolic universe which expressed the longing of late-nineteenth-century women that the matriarchal world of the mothers be sustained. By her use of "imaginative realism" she carried the themes of the earlier local colorists to a powerful and complex conclusion. Hers is perhaps the last fully female-identified vision in women's literature. For later women writers such as Wharton, Cather, and Gertrude Stein, the world of men was too much with them for this kind of imaginative construction. Jewett's vision, therefore, remains a powerful response to the transitions that were happening in women's lives at the turn of the century. Mary E. Wilkins Freeman formulated another, more extreme.

8

Mary E. Wilkins Freeman and the Tree of Knowledge

Something is dying in the fictional world of Mary E. Wilkins Freeman. A way of life—the woman-centered, matriarchal world of the Victorians—is in its last throes. The preindustrial values of that world, female-identified and ecologically holistic, are going down to defeat before the imperialism of masculine technology and patriarchal institutions. In Sarah Orne Jewett's vision the world of the mothers holds its own against the historical forces that impend its demise. With Mary E. Wilkins Freeman the mothers are taking a last stand, going down to apparently inevitable defeat. The hopelessness of their prospect drives many of them to a kind of obsessive protectiveness of their daughters; at times their behavior becomes almost perversely destructive.

Freeman, the last of the New England local color school, came close to a modernist sensibility. In many of her stories she seems to have distilled the local color topos down to its essence. One has often a sense of a script of gestures reduced to mechanical repetition, as if the heart or soul had been removed, as if somehow the meaning had vacated. The sense of the absurd, of a metaphysically sparse environment is very strong in these works. But it is not "God" who is dead or dying in the world of Mary E. Wilkins Freeman; it is the Mother and a woman-centered world.

Like Jewett Freeman employed "imaginative realism" (although perhaps less consciously so); she turned rural New England into a symbolic landscape whose moral events signified the state of women entering the twentieth century. Many of her stories have an aesthetic purity that give them great power. At her best Freeman created master stories equal to those of Chekhov, or indeed, of her teacher, Sarah Orne Jewett.

"The Tree of Knowledge" (*The Love of Parson Lord and Other Stories* 1900) is a paradigmatic mother–daughter script. In this case the relationship is between sisters Cornelia, an older, protective figure, and Annie Pryor.

For years Cornelia had written fictitious love letters to Annie, signing them "David Amicus." Her idea was that she would create so pure an ideal of manhood in Annie's mind that she would never succumb to ordinary men's wiles. Her plans are thwarted, however, when Annie, in the fashion of the female quixote, naively greets a prowler as her ideal beau. Cornelia manages to repair the situation by revealing her scheme to the intruder (another "burglar in paradise"), who is so moved that he vows to prove himself worthy of Annie's faith. This he does, and they marry, much to Cornelia's chagrin. She then wonders "if it might not sometimes be better to guard the Tree of Knowledge with the flaming sword, instead of the gates of a lost Paradise."[1]

Once again we find a woman writer of the late nineteenth century using biblical images of the fall to convey the historically induced ambivalence women were feeling about leaving their traditional female sanctuaries and going out into a male-dominated world. As we noted in the last chapter in the discussion of "A White Heron," and in the chapter on Elizabeth Stuart Phelps, the female sanctuary was perceived as a paradise and the threat to that paradise was male intrusion. That Freeman presents the paradise as "lost" and the threat as "the Tree of Knowledge" correlates with the historical transitions noted above. In Freeman's view, however, these transitions are much further along than heretofore; the situation is much more desperate and much more extreme measures are required to deal with it—perhaps an accurate expression of her historical moment.

While some might be tempted to impose a sexual interpretation on this imagery, and construe the women's resistance as a fear of male sexuality, such a reading does not explain why this imagery appears at a particular *historical* moment and not before. For it is only in the late nineteenth century, beginning among these writers with Phelps (and not seen in Cooke or Stowe), that one begins to sense a *fear* that the female sanctuary may be destroyed—not so much by male sexuality per se but by the forces of masculine knowledge, by industrialism, by patriarchal governmental and educational institutions. This is quite different from the rape-and-destroy motif seen in the "heroine's text." Consequently it seems that the only valid explanation for the emergence of the "destruction-of-paradise" theme in women's literature must lie in these historical factors. The backwater matriarchal pockets of rural New England are being destroyed by rapid transportation and communication systems, and women in significant numbers for the first time in history are entering male educational institutions, bastions of androcentric analytic knowledge—the antithesis of the kind of matriarchal and holistic knowledge promoted in, for example, *The Country of the Pointed Firs* or "A White Heron."

Freeman's attitude toward this dying world is ambivalent. On the one hand the mothers—perhaps in some sense a part of every woman's psyche—are trying to keep their daughters "home," in a female world. The daughters, however, at least sometimes are interested in exploring realities beyond the home. The daughters' feelings are perhaps best summed up in a semi-autobiographical story Freeman never finished: "I am a graft on the tree of human womanhood. I am a hybrid. Sometimes I think I am a monster, and the worst of it is, I certainly take pleasure in it."[2] Indeed one senses that the author's ambivalent insider-outsider status, which is endemic to local color literature, here takes on the added dimension of a mother–daughter rift. Perhaps this was always the case: the daughter–author positing herself in relationship to her own mother, who was inevitably the quintessential insider.

Freeman, more than the earlier local colorists, distanced herself from her own environment, and wrote more as an outsider, even though she knew that rural world from within. In her 1899 Introduction to *Pembroke* (1894) she demonstrates her dual focus, noting that only "the initiated" can know the inner realities of rural life, to which "the sojourner from cities for the summer months cannot often penetrate in the least." For: "There is often to a mind from the outside world an almost repulsive narrowness and a pitiful sordidness which amounts to tragedy in the lives of such people . . . but quite generally the tragedy exists only in the comprehension of the observer and not at all in that of the observed."[3]

More than a score of Freeman's stories and novels deal with the mother–daughter bond or with similarly intense relationships between women. Although unnoted by earlier commentators, it is one of the dominant themes in her work. Four stories in her first published collection, *A Humble Romance and Other Stories* (1887), deal with such relationships.

"A Modern Dragon" concerns parental blockage of a young couple's romance—another dominant Freeman theme. One of the mothers, however, becomes so worried about her daughter's welfare that she dies of exhaustion. On her deathbed her daughter cries: "Oh, mother! mother! mother! . . . I do love you best! I always will! I never will love him as much as I did you. I promise you" (77).

In "Brakes and White Vi'lets," a particularly touching story, an elderly spinster, Marm Lawson, is deprived of a beloved granddaughter whom she has tended for ten years, when her father decides the Lawson house is too damp for the girl, and removes her. It is a plot that anticipates Freeman's tragic story "Old Woman Magoun," discussed below. The girl is, therefore, taken out of a female sanctuary "for her own good," against the wishes of the matriarchal figure. Marm thus has to choose whether to move with the child into alien surroundings or to remain in her familiar and dear world, signified by the "brakes and white vi'lets" that grow around the house. Reluctantly she decides to move in order to be near the girl, but death claims her before that can be accomplished.

"A Gatherer of Simples" is also about a threatened mother–daughter relationship. Aurelia Flower, a "yarb-woman," or herb gatherer, has unofficially adopted a neighboring orphan. Both are very happy with the arrangement, but one day the child's natural grandmother comes to take her away. Heartbroken, Aurelia hands her over; however, the tale ends happily when the girl runs back to Aurelia and the grandmother dies.

Like the preceding two stories "A Far-Away Melody" is a simple, sad, and touching story that seems stripped down to a moral essence. It concerns twin sisters who are devoted to one another. When one of them dies the other is desolate. "This sister-love was all she had ever felt . . . all the passion of devotion of which this homely, commonplace woman was capable was centered in that, and the unsatisfied strength of it was killing her" (217).

Two of the stories in Freeman's next collection, *A New England Nun and Other Stories* (1891) also concern mother–daughter relationships. "An Innocent Gamester" shows how an overprotective will can become tyrannical. Aunt Lucinda, with whom Charlotte has come to live, forbids her her favorite pastime, fortune-telling by cards. Charlotte, nearly overcome by Lucinda's nagging, runs away, which scares Lucinda into realizing how oppressive she has been.

In "Amanda and Love" Amanda is the older sister, but she is old enough to be Love's mother, and the two have lived together alone since Love's birth. Amanda breaks off a courtship between Love and Willis Dale, but guiltily restores it after she realizes that Love is pining away. As the two resume courting, Amanda leaves the room and weeps silently in the kitchen.

Several other stories recount the self-sacrifice of one woman's happiness to ensure the happiness of another. In these painful cases the ties between the women are often stronger than those between the woman and the intruding man, or the "beau." Where Jewett's women would have resisted the man, affirming thereby the validity of their own bond, Freeman's seem driven by another moral compulsion: they assume the male imperative is the greater. And where they choose to resist, they are driven to adopt measures far more extreme than any imaginable in Jewett's world (see especially "Old Woman Magoun" and "The Long Arm").

In "A Moral Exigency" (*A Humble Romance,* 1887) Eunice Fairweather relinquishes her suitor to another woman, Ada Harris, after she remembers how she had played with Ada as a child "and that golden head had nestled on her bosom" (231). When she announces her decision Eunice draws "that golden head" against her again and says, "Love me all you can, Ada . . . I—want something" (233).

Araminta White is similarly noble in "The Chance of Araminta" (*The Givers* 1904). She gives up her beau when she learns he had earlier been engaged to another. There is in this story, as in "A New England Nun," the suggestion that she is better off without him. "I told her maybe she'd never have another chance, and she said if she did she'd never take it . . ." (225). "'Well, marriage ain't everything,' said the cousin" (226).

By the Light of the Soul (1907), a novel, relates a nearly suicidal gesture of self-sacrifice of one sister for her half sister. Maria Edgham, again much older than her sibling, is obsessively fond of younger Evelyn. "She . . . reflected how much more she loved Evelyn than she loved George Ramsey [a suitor], how much more precious a little, innocent, beautiful girl was than a man."[4] Evelyn confides, in return, "I love you so, Maria, that I don't feel well" (353). Their bond, however, is threatened when, in an improbable sequence of events, they both find themselves in love with the same man. Maria nobly backs off, leaves town, and even has a false death notice printed up. Happily, however, on her departing journey she has met another woman, a dwarf, with whom she eventually shares a home and develops a mother–daughter relationship similar to the one she has just relinquished. "The poor little dwarf seemed the very child of her heart" (498).

Two other minor stories develop these themes. "The Reign of the Doll" (*The Givers*) deals with the reconciliation of two sisters, and "Lucy" (*The Givers*) is about two grandparents' dismay when their granddaughter is lost on a visit to Boston. The tension between urban and rural is marked here and the journey of the young girl is in some way symbolic of the "journeys" women are making from their rural sanctuaries into urban "modern" civilization. This girl returns safely to her rural retreat.

The Portion of Labor (1901), ostensibly a social novel about factory conditions and working-class miseries, is really on another and deeper level a work about a young woman's ambivalence about her proper role. Ellen Brewster is one of the first "modern" women to appear in local color fiction. Though she comes from a working-class background, she excels in school, is valedictorian of her high school class, and is bound for Vassar. She is on the verge of escaping from not only her class background but also from the traditional female role of wife and mother that go with it. But Ellen has reservations: ". . . she wondered if she ought to go to college, and maybe gain thereby a career which was beyond anything her own loved ones had known."[5]

Ellen's dilemma is dramatized through two sets of opposing characters. On the one side are her own mother and father, worn down by the oppressive conditions that rule their lives. Of their sort is Granville Joy, a working-class suitor, who can offer her little more than a repetition of her mother's drudgery-filled life. Significantly, Ellen becomes irritated with Granville's use of dialect, especially "ain't"—a tension we have seen throughout local color literature. On the other hand are wealthy friends Ellen has become fond of: Cynthia Lennox, who has offered to put her through college, and Cynthia's nephew, Robert, another suitor, who in the course of the novel becomes the owner of the shoe factory where her father works. This may seem to be a variation of the two-suitors convention seen in Jewett's novel *A Marsh Island* (1884),[6] in which a rural girl properly chooses a rural suitor over an urban one. But in Freeman's novel the convention is complicated by Ellen's infatuation with Cynthia. The lesbian nature of that relationship becomes clear in the following passage:

She had so hoped she might find Cynthia alone [Robert was with her]. She had dreamed, as a lover might have done, of a tête-à-tête with her, what she would say, what Cynthia would say. She had thought, and trembled at the thought, that possibly Cynthia might kiss her when she came or went. She had felt, with a thrill of spirit, the touch of Cynthia's soft lips on hers, she had smelt the violets about her clothes. Now it was all spoiled (268).

This relationship is not, however, developed in the novel. In fact it is dropped rather inexplicably in the novel's rush of events. (One of the flaws in Freeman's novels indeed is a tendency to proliferate characters, events, and motives without carefully tying them all together.) Instead, familial financial troubles force Ellen to abandon her hopes of going to college. She must become a factory worker. The novel then devolves into a romance between Ellen and Robert, with her class loyalties and a strike threatening to prevent their happy ending. But all is artificially resolved, class barriers are forgotten, at the novel's end. Nevertheless, in her loyalty to and empathy with the workers, which at times becomes mystical, Ellen reveals a deep identification with the oppressed and in that sense affirms that her proper role is with them.

Ellen reaches a kind of compromise solution, therefore, to the dilemma of whether to leave the traditional world, which is seen negatively as providing limited opportunities for women. In marrying Robert rather than Granville she does move beyond the situation of her mother; however, she also chooses marriage rather than a relationship with Cynthia, which is now represented as something rather exotic. And she chooses to remain in her home environment rather than to go off to the new urban world of opportunities and dangers accorded women by the turn of the century.

"Sister Liddy" (*A New England Nun*), one of Freeman's classics, is also of paradigmatic significance when seen in the context of women's literary traditions: it is perhaps the ultimate ironic portrayal of the sentimental heroine. For, what give meaning to the lives of the women in the poorhouse are the stories they tell of past glories.

One woman, Polly Moss, who is old and badly crippled, speaks rapturously of her sister, Liddy. Liddy was everything that Polly was not; she was beautiful, she had married well, she had a big trousseau, lived in a fashionable apartment in Boston, etc. She was in short a personification of the sentimental ideal. When pressed as to why Liddy has allowed her sister to fall into such unfortunate circumstances, Polly acknowledges that she is dead. Nevertheless, she remains for Polly a kind of deity, a justification for her own misery. "Old Polly Moss, her little withered face gleaming with reckless enthusiasm, sang the praises of her sister Liddy as wildly and faithfully as any minnesinger his angel mistress" (96). On Polly's own deathbed she acknowledges further that Liddy was a creation of her own dreams.

That the sentimental ideal has been reduced to a fantasy in the mind of a pathetic old woman brings to a rather grim conclusion the anti-romance tendency we have traced through this study. And that the sustaining sister/lover is now perceived as but a fabricated illusion is another and powerful expression of the process of "the fall" that was happening in women's culture.

Jane Field (1893), a novel published shortly after "Sister Liddy," again concerns a mother–daughter relationship. In this case the mother is driven to crime to protect her daughter's welfare. Lois Field, the daughter, is consumptive, and everyone says she needs a vacation to recover, but Jane, the mother, cannot afford it. Jane's sister, Esther, had also died of consumption, so Jane is especially anxious about Lois. In a somewhat improbable plot Jane manages to convince the executors of a will that she is Esther. Thus she obtains the money for Lois. Lois, however, resents her mother's illegal machinations, and especially the duplicity it requires when she has to lie to a suitor. The mother finally repents, admits her crime, but remains somewhat addled, while Lois marries her beau.

Freeman was interested in the psychology of otherwise good persons being driven to criminal acts, usually robbery, under the pressure of (usually) economic circumstances. Other stories that depict this phenomenon include: "Calla-Lillies and Hannah" (*A New England Nun*), "A Stolen Christmas" (*A New England Nun*), "The Last Gift" (*The Givers*), and "The Winning Lady" (*The Winning Lady and Others* 1909).

Pembroke (1894), a powerful novel about a series of intractable New England wills in conflict, also presents one of Freeman's most dramatic examples of the domineering, overprotective mother in Deborah

Thayer, who is said to watch over her daughter Rebecca "with a fierce, pecking tenderness like a bird."[7] When she suspects Rebecca of being pregnant, however, she throws her out, and refuses to see her again, even when the baby dies. After this Deborah becomes even more dictatorial over her son, Ephraim. One day, when she discovers that he has been playing instead of working, she beats him. The stress is too much for his already diseased body and he dies. The stress of this event is too much for her and she too dies shortly thereafter of a stroke.

"Evelina's Garden" (*Silence and Other Stories* 1898) is one of the most significant stories in this study. As a reversal of the theme of Jewett's "A White Heron" it serves as a further and powerful illustration of society's shifting values. An elderly woman, Evelina Adams, has maintained her garden for years as a kind of female sanctuary. When she dies she bequeaths it and the rest of her estate to her niece, also named Evelina. The terms of the will, however, are that young Evelina must perpetuate the garden and must never marry. Evelina is willing to forgo her inheritance in order to marry her suitor, but he is poor and refuses to allow her to do so. She decides that the only way she can win him over is to destroy the garden, thereby being disinherited. This she does by ripping up all the plants—pouring boiling water and salt on the roots—"all the time weeping, and moaning softly: 'Poor Cousin Evelina! poor Cousin Evelina! oh, forgive me, poor cousin Evelina !'" (179).

Here we have a painfully graphic image of destruction of a natural realm which is a quintessentially female world. That this destruction is deemed necessary in order for the girl to go over to the male world suggests that "Evelina's Garden" is a symbolic representation of the fundamental historical transitions that are happening in women's lives; it is a repetition of the destruction-of-paradise motif.

"The Love of Parson Lord" (*The Love of Parson Lord*) is another of Freeman's stories that seem to have many conflicting stands that do not entirely knit together. Nevertheless, it also depicts a strong mother–daughter bond. In this case the mother-figure is a neighboring woman who is something of a beneficent benefactress and benign diety combined. When Love Lord (that is the girl's name) first sees the woman in church she becomes "conscious of nothing except that mother-presence, which seemed to pervade the whole church. The inexorable fatherhood of God . . . was not as evident to [her] as the

motherhood of the squire's lady. She continued to gaze at her . . . with
. . . eyes of adoration . . ." (14). She felt "a sort of ecstasy, as of first
love" (23). Love's father was a typical Calvinistic minister, a throw-
back to some of Cooke's and Stowe's caricatures, harsh, unbending,
given to a meager Spartan life. Under the influence of the woman,
however, he relents. The story devolves into a romance between Love
and the woman's grandson, Robert, whose main attraction to the girl
seems to be his connection to his grandmother.

The Shoulders of Atlas (1908), a novel, is one of Freeman's most intriguing works, although it too can be faulted for incongruities and in-
consistencies. The novel depicts several intense relationships between
women. The central relationship is that between Sylvia Whitman and
Rose Fletcher. Sylvia and her husband, Henry, had inherited an estate
and income late in life when a distant relative, Abrahama White, died.
Rose, a niece of Abrahama's, comes to town when a childhood guardian of hers, Eliza Farrell, dies under mysterious circumstances. Rose
stays with the Whitmans, and the bond between her and Sylvia grows
into a quasi-lesbian, quasi-mother–daugher relationship.

Eliza, too, had had lesbian tendencies ("I think she loved women
better than a woman usually does"[8]). And she also had been overprotective of Rose; indeed, had feared sending her to boarding schools lest
she form "one of those erotic friendships, which are really diseased love-
affairs, with another girl or a teacher . . ." (158).

The relationship between Sylvia and Rose intensifies during Rose's
stay. Sylvia "adored the girl to such an extent that the adoration fairly
pained her" (109). Rose "coquetted with this older woman who loved
her, and whom she loved, with that charming coquettishness sometimes seen in a daughter towards her mother" (109). When Rose at-
tracts a suitor, Sylvia does her utmost to interfere with the courtship.
Henry and a friend discuss Sylvia's behavior:

"Maybe Sylvia is in love with the girl," said Meeks, shrewdly.
"I know she is," said Henry. ". . . but I have always understood that moth-
ers were crazy to have their daughters married."
"So have I, but these popular ideas are sometimes nonsense" (261).

Sylvia finally reveals that her "odd" behavior toward Rose had been
motivated by a mistaken belief that Rose was the proper heir of the
White estate. But this is an insufficient resolution. Sylvia is simply

forced to give Rose up because the moral imperative in the novel is male-identified. Like the later Elizabeth Stuart Phelps, Mary E. Wilkins Freeman seems to have imbibed a moral atmosphere which assumes the male prerogative. This helps to explain the incongruity we have noted in her plots—especially in her novels *The Portion of Labor* and *By the Light of the Soul*—where intense relationships between women are simply dropped with no explanation, as if no explanation were needed, as if no one would or could question the superiority of the male claim to women's affection, attention, and commitment. Still Freeman does depict the unresolved female liaisons, something that later writers like Wharton, Cather, and Stein chose for the most part to ignore, repress, or disguise.

In *The Shoulders of Atlas* there is another, more peculiar relationship between women, that between a minor character, Lucy, and her mother. Lucy is suspected of having poisoned Eliza Farrell because she feared Eliza was stealing her beau; however, this proves not to be the case. Lucy's mother is another of the overprotective breed; mainly she is terrified that Lucy will behave in an unseemly manner, since the girl is "man-crazy." Despite this orientation an unexplained flirtation develops between Lucy and Rose. Lucy claims at one point, "I can make you blush, looking at you, as if I were a man" (140). Nonetheless, both Lucy and Rose end up marrying men—in an ending that seems contrived.

Three final Freeman stories will conclude this discussion of the mother–daughter relationship in her work. Each of them provides a paradigmatic resolution to the psychic dilemma we have seen as endemic to the female sensitivities of the time: whether to leave the female sanctuary, how to keep it intact, how to protect the mother-daughter bond, how to keep relationships between women from being destroyed by the male intruder, himself emblematic of the turn-of-the-century reassertion of destructive patriarchal knowledge.

The title character in "Arethusa" (*Understudies* 1901) like her namesake in classical mythology is a shy, reclusive girl, unresponsive to suitors, who does not want to leave her mother. "I don't like men. I am afraid of them. I want to stay with you" (155). Her favorite pastime is to visit the arethusa flower, which grows only in a sheltered, reclusive area of the swamp, another image of the female sanctuary. Under the pressure of circumstances she finally agrees, reluctantly, to marry. On her wedding day she is missing; they find her on one last visit to the arethusa in the swamp. She does marry and has children, but every spring she sneaks away alone to visit the arethusa. Her husband indulges this whim, never "dreaming that it had its roots in the very depths of her nature, and that she perhaps sought this fair neutral ground of the flower kingdom as a refuge from the exigency of life" (169).

"The Long Arm" (*The Long Arm* 1895) is a detective story that presents another, more chilling response to the female dilemma. Phoebe Dole, a spinster dressmaker, has lived with Maria Woods for over forty years. Phoebe is overprotective of Maria to the point of being tyrannical. When a neighbor, Fairbanks, is found murdered, no one suspects Phoebe until evidence accumulates that points in her direction. She finally confesses. Maria and the neighbor had been engaged forty years before and Phoebe had forced Maria to break off the engagement. The neighbor had then married another, who had recently died. Fairbanks was evidently pressing his suit again when Phoebe felt compelled once more to interfere, this time by murder. In her confession she notes: "[Maria] was going to marry [him]—I found it out. I stopped it once before. This time I knew I couldn't unless I killed him. She's lived with me in that house for over forty years. There are other ties as strong as the marriage one, that are just as sacred. What right had he to take her away from me and break up my home?"[9]

"Old Woman Magoun" (*The Winning Lady*), a justly celebrated tale, brings to tragic culmination the issue of the paradisiacal female sanctuary. The plot concerns a confrontation between "Old Woman Magoun" and Nelson Berry over custody of her granddaughter, Lily, who is his daughter. Lily's mother had died when Lily was an infant. The father, who allegedly had married the mother and deserted her, had paid little attention to Lily for fourteen years. The old woman had brought her up and loves her dearly. Together they form a female home. The old woman is zealous about maintaining that home free from men, and is somewhat overprotective of the girl. She sees men as the enemy:

> "It seems queer to me . . . that men can't do nothin' without havin' to drink and chew to keep their spirits up. . . ."
> "Men is different," said Sally Jinks.
> "Yes, they be," asserted Old Woman Magoun, with open contempt (244–45).

Later she thinks, ". . . they air a passel of hogs" (258).

One day Nelson comes to demand custody of the girl. The grandmother suspects that he is going to turn her over to a gambling partner to pay off a debt; in other words, that he is going to turn her over to prostitution—a suspicion that is somewhat corroborated by Berry's behavior. The grandmother desperately tries to have the girl adopted by a wealthy couple in a nearby town, but to no avail. On the journey over, the old woman says, "Grandma . . . wouldn't hurt you for nothin', except it was to save your life . . ." (266). On the way home, the girl eats some poisonous berries of the deadly nightshade plant; the grandmother does nothing to stop her, knowing full well that the child will die. As Lily is dying, her grandmother describes the paradise she will enter at death. It is another image of the female sanctuary: ". . . a beautiful place, where the flowers grow tall" (273). There "you [will] find your mother, and she will take you home . . ." (275).

In addition to her treatment of mothers and daughters Freeman carried on a local color tradition by creating a gallery of strong female characters, some of whom adopted traditionally masculine professions, some of whom exerted themselves in "unfeminine" ways, often to the point of personal rebellion or revolt.

One of the most outstanding of these is "Christmas Jenny" (*A New England Nun*). The title figure is of the local colorists' breed of matriarchal nature-women. Jenny Wrayne lives up on a mountain in a "weather-beaten hut" which she shares with scores of injured wild animals and birds and with a deaf-mute boy she has adopted. Like Sylvia in "A White Heron," "Christmas Jenny" is at home in the woods and protects its inhabitants against destructive male intruders. When asked what Jenny does with all the birds and animals in her house, a friend explains her mission:

"Does with 'em? Well, I'll tell you what she does with 'em. She picks 'em up in the woods when they're starvin' and freezin' an' half dead, an' she brings 'em in here, an' takes care of 'em an' feeds 'em till they gets well, an' then she lets 'em go again. . . . You see that rabbit there? Well, he's been in a trap. Somebody wanted to kill the poor little cretur. You see that robin? Somebody fired a gun at him an' broke his wing" (172).

The town patriarchs become suspicious of Jenny and her menagerie and talk of institutionalizing her, but a woman friend strongly defends her and deflects the men from their purpose. The narrator observes that the men perceive Jenny as a witch and their attack on her is a witch-hunt. "Everything out of the broad, common track was a horror to these men. . . . The popular sentiment against Jenny Wrayne was originally . . . a remnant of the old New England witchcraft superstition. More than anything else, Jenny's eccentricity, her possibly uncanny deviation from the ordinary . . . had brought this inquiry upon her. In actual meaning . . . it was a witch-hunt" (174).

The story repeats the pattern of the woman preserving her natural, female sanctuary against patriarchal destruction. As in "A White Heron," such destruction is posed in terms of hunting and trapping, mechanized masculine operations that destroy that natural life with which the women identify. Freeman dealt with the witch craze in other works, notably "Silence" and "The Little Maid at the Door" (both in *Silence and Other Stories*) and in *Giles Corey, Yeoman: A Play* (1893).

Several stories of less importance also depict memorable women engaged in heroic tasks. "A Humble Romance" (*A Humble Romance*) portrays a woman who successfully adopts her husband's trade of tin-peddling. "An Old Arithmetician" (*A Humble Romance*) is about a woman obsessed with "ciphering." "A Wayfaring Couple" (*A New England Nun*) presents a Sisyphean image of a woman who, to save her husband's life, puts the traces of a sulky carriage on herself and pulls him three miles to a doctor. "Louisa" (*A New England Nun*) is about a woman who does men's field labor to support her family. *Madelon* (1896) concerns a woman who kills a man but whose lover is imprisoned in her stead because no one believes a woman could have committed the deed. Madelon then spends her time securing her lover's release.

In several stories the woman's heroics consist in rejecting a suitor. The most celebrated of these is the much-anthologized "A New England Nun" (*A New England Nun*). This story, too, recounts the preservation of a male-less female sanctuary against a male intruder. Louisa Ellis and Joe Dagget have been engaged for fourteen years while he made his fortune in Australia. Upon his return she realizes that he will destroy the order and neatness of her peaceful existence, and they agree mutually to break the engagement. The author's ambivalence is clear in this story; a caged canary and a tied-up dog symbolize the price Louisa must pay for order and security: eternal restriction to a limited sphere.

"A Symphony in Lavender" (*A Humble Romance*) also concerns a spinster who rejects a suitor. She does so because of a prophetic dream in which a man approaches and asks for one of her flowers. She is about to give him one when a white dove lands on her shoulder. The man suddenly looks "at once beautiful and repulsive" (45); she flees. Later, when a similar episode happens in real life, a "horror of him" comes over her, and she chooses to live her life out alone. Here as in "A White Heron" a white bird seems to symbolize a female force, one that urges the preservation of the female realm. We have noted that in the Grimm version of "Cinderella" the white bird is the spirit of the girl's mother.

"A Taste of Honey" (*A Humble Romance*) also involves the rejection of a suitor, but for other reasons. Inez Morse has vowed to pay off her father's mortgage and refuses to marry until she does so. Her suitor waits for a while but gives up and marries another just before her debt is paid. She refuses to mourn, however, and is proud of her accomplishment.

A number of Freeman women are moved to active rebellion in order to protect their own interests. The most famous of these stories is "The Revolt of 'Mother'" (*A New England Nun*), which portrays a male–female confrontation in which the woman wins her way through a tactic of nonviolent resistance. Adoniram Penn is a silent patriarch who will listen to no reason other than his own. His wife, Sarah, has been promised a new house for forty years. When Adoniram begins to build a new barn, she is enraged, and while he is away moves all her furniture into the barn, does some remodeling, and turns it into the new house she has always wanted.

Significantly, Mary E. Wilkins Freeman recanted this story in 1917. She wrote: "There never was in New England a woman like Mother. If there had been she certainly would not have moved into the palatial barn. . . . She simply would have lacked the nerve. She would also have lacked the imagination."[10] How far we are in 1917 from the heroic mothers of Stowe and Jewett.

Two stories from *A Humble Romance* (1887) also depict minor revolts. One is "Cinnamon Roses" where a woman prevents a man from destroying some favorite roses; the other, "A Mistaken Charity," concerns the flight of two elderly sisters from a poorhouse back to their own home. Two later stories—"Bouncing Bet" (*Understudies*) and "The Elm Tree" (*Six Trees* 1903)—similarly portray successful resistance to the poorhouse. "A Village Singer" and "A Church Mouse," both in *A New England Nun,* also concern spirited and successful tactics of revolt.

"One Good Time" (*The Love of Parson Lord*) relates the humorous fling of Narcissa Stone, who, after scrimping and saving all her life and after years of paternal oppression, takes off for a "good time" in New York City before settling down to marriage. Her fiancé is mystified but she explains: "If I had to settle down in your house, as I have done in father's, and see the years stretching ahead like a long road without any turn, and nothing but the same old dog-trot of washing and ironing and scrubbing and cooking and sewing and washing dishes till I drop into my grave, I should hate you, William Crane" (213).

The momentary repudiation of the female role is really an assertion of her own spirit of independence and quest for knowledge. "I 'ain't never done anything my whole life that I thought I ought not to do, but now I'm going to." And: "I've just drudged, drudged ever since I can remember. . . . I don't know anything but my own tracks, and—I'm going to get out of them for a while . . ." (210). "Love ain't enough sometimes when it ties anybody. Everybody has got their own feet and their own wanting to use 'em, and sometimes when love comes in the way of that, it ain't anything but a dead wall. . . . I tell you . . . I've got to jump my wall, and I've got to have one good time" (213). So, significantly, Narcissa rejects the traditional female world of love and drudgery in favor of another, more exciting world, and of new knowledge. This is the daughter speaking.

Another strong story of revolt is "The Balsam Fir" (*Six Trees*). Martha Elder, an embittered spinster, has over the years developed a "strong . . . spirit of rebellion against the small-ness of her dole of the good things of life" (104). "Her own tracks, which were apparently those of peace, [were] in reality those of a caged panther" (111). Her one possession is a beautiful balsam fir that grows in front of her house. One evening shortly before Christmas a woodsman comes to chop it down. She tears out of the house, grabs his axe, and threatens to kill him if he does. Wisely, he departs. The episode helps to open Martha up to a deaf woman who has been visiting; she invites her to remain for an extended stay. Though the story is presented through Christian symbolism, we see once again that the underlying pattern is of a female realm being threatened with destruction by a male intruder; and once again the natural world is preserved by the woman in a nearly violent gesture of revolt.

In most of Freeman's stories one has a sense of a world that has out-lived its time and of people who have been too long isolated from the communal mainstream. We noted a similar sense of disenchantment with rural life as early as Rose Terry Cooke, but in Cooke and Jewett the meager circumstances at least sometimes combined to create ad-mirable strength of character. In Freeman's view, however, there is often no mitigating justification for the emptiness of these lives. In her relentless depiction of the vanity of these existences she is strikingly modern.

"A Traveling Sister" (*The Winning Lady*) and "A Patient Waiter" (*A Humble Romance*) could perhaps be grouped with "Sister Liddy" to signify the death of the romance tradition. In the first story two of the three Allerton sisters have always vacationed together while the third has always gone off on a secret romantic voyage which for years has mystified the other two. After she dies they discover in her diary that she has always stayed home; her "voyage" has been to put on old dresses and to stare at mementos of her long-dead lover. "A Patient Waiter" is a kind of local colorist version of Samuel Beckett's twen-tieth-century drama *Waiting For Godot*. Fidelia Almy had gone to the post office twice a day for forty years for a letter from her lover, Ansel Lennox, who had gone West to earn money for their marriage. Finally she dies, having spent her life waiting for a redemption that never came.

"A Poetess" (*A New England Nun*) is another classic and tragic story about pathetic waste. Betsey Dole is an impoverished, half-starved spinster whose entire obsession in life is with writing poetry. Her con-fidence in her calling is completely undermined when she learns that the local minister, also an amateur poet, thinks her poems are worth-less. Betsey is devastated by the cruel irony of it: "Had I ought to have been born with the wantin' to write poetry if I couldn't write it—had I? Had I ought to have been let to write all my life, an' not know before there wa'n't any use in it? Would it be fair if that canary-bird there, that ain't never done anything but sing, should turn out not to be singin'?" (154–55). However, despite this painful protest, she burns all her work, puts the ashes in a jar, and when she is dying asks that it be buried with her. The story anticipates Kafka's "A Hunger Artist," which also suggests the problematic nature of religious devotion to any calling. But it also seems peculiarly representative of untold numbers of failed women artists whose works have been lost to history.

"An Honest Soul" (*A Humble Romance*) similarly depicts a woman compelled to complete her craft properly, but in this story the compulsion comes more directly from her inherited Calvinistic conscience. Martha Patch, another impoverished spinster, survives by making quilts and doing odd sewing jobs. Once, while doing a quilting job for two people at once, she gets the wrong squares in the wrong quilt and has to take them off. When she finds she has repeated her error, she painstakingly repeats the whole laborious process. Meanwhile her stores of food are low, and her task has severely exhausted her. The narrator comments that it is her own false pride—which derives from a Calvinistic sense of paying one's way—that has led to this impasse. "There was really no necessity for such a state of things; she was surrounded by kindly well-to-do people, who would have gone themselves rather than let her suffer. But she . . . felt great pride about accepting anything for which she did not pay" (86).

Most critics of Freeman's work have focused on the theme of the intractable New England will become destructive. In her Introduction to *Pembroke* Freeman gives a brief anecdote to illustrate how she perceived the calcification of the will as a central "disease" in the New England of her day:

There lived in a New England village . . . a man who objected to the painting of the kitchen floor, and who quarreled furiously with his wife concerning the same. When she persisted, in spite of his wishes to the contrary, and the floor was painted, he refused to cross it to his dying day, and always, to his great inconvenience, but probably to his soul's satisfaction, walked around it.[11]

Freeman carried on the anti-Calvinist tradition of her predecessors. Implicit in her work is a plea for a relaxation of such mindless tyrannies as depicted in the above anecdote and for the establishment of a more humane treatment of self and others. In Freeman's work, nevertheless, the authoritarian figure is less often a Calvinistic minister and more often a patriarch within: an exacting conscience that forces one to live up to a compulsive standard. Freeman detected the fundamental paradox in Calvinism—the idea that grace could somehow be *forced* by an exertion of individual will. Freeman shows, in her later works especially, that grace occurs independently of the will and, as often as not, only when the will ceases and desists. In this sense she brings to culmination the local colorists' concern with the issue of grace versus works. Unlike her predecessors she is clearly skeptical about the efficacity of works. Again one may tie this to the sense of a fall, a sense of resignation, or a failure of nerve that seems to characterize the female psyche of the time.

In Freeman's view the overpowering will is a destructive force. Often the form taken by stories with this theme is that of a romance thwarted by parental tenacity. One of the most interesting of these from the point of view of continuing women's traditions is "The Buckley Lady" (*Silence and Other Stories*). This story is somewhat reminiscent of Stowe's classic repudiation of the European romance, "A Yankee Girl" (see chapter 4). Set in Colonial times, it concerns the attempts by parents, Ichabod and Sarah Buckley, to turn their daughter into a "lady" so that she may marry a wealthy European aristocrat. "All the Buckley family seemed to have united in a curious reversed tyranny towards this beautiful child" (70). She is no longer allowed to go barefoot, she must keep her hands and face shaded from the sun, she learns the piano and how to dance, she is given *Clarissa* to read—all preparation for becoming a lady. The years wear on and no gentleman appears. It begins to look as if all the efforts have been in vain. However, the girl finally subverts her parents' will: she and her American suitor arrange that he arrive in a coach and four, dressed as a gentleman. This fools the father and so the young couple marries.

Many of the Freeman stories that deal with this theme, of course, are more than just romances. Like Jewett, Freeman seems concerned to present a kind of moral humanism. The softening of the tyrannical patriarchal will leads to a rebirth of human potential, to a renewal of the human community, which is sustained by such maternal values as charity and compassion. Three stories seem to best illustrate this important theme. Significantly, perhaps, two of them concern men. The first, "An Innocent Gamester," discussed above, shows how the relaxation of a tyrannically condemnatory conscience leads to the renewal of a relationship between two women.

The second, "A Solitary" (*A New England Nun*), is about a male version of Jewett's hermit-woman, Joanna. Nicholas Gunn had lived a life of self-flagellation ever since his wife ran off with another man. He eats nothing but cornmeal and refuses to heat his cabin in the depths of winter. Stephen Forster, a feeble consumptive, staggers by regularly on his way to town. Only reluctantly does Nicholas even let him rest in his cabin. One night, however, Stephen comes to the door; he is freezing and in need of immediate attention. Somehow the sight of this pathetic soul opens Nicholas up. He starts a fire, feeds him, covers him with blankets, and begins to "rub him under the bedclothes. His face was knit savagely, but he rubbed with a tender strength" (226). Stephen had been running away for fear of being sent to the poorhouse. Nicholas agrees to take him in permanently, and to share his life with him. The relaxation of Nicholas's rigid regime allows him to experience once again the warmth of human companionship.

"The Great Pine" is another of the symbolist stories in *Six Trees* (1903) which show the moral effect of natural objects on human behavior. In this work a ne'er-do-well man, wandering in the woods, becomes angry with a great pine and decides to set it afire—another example of male destructive violence against the natural world. Something calls him back, however; he puts out the fire and saves the tree. Shortly after, he returns to the family he had deserted years before. He finds his wife dead, her second husband barely alive, with his children. All are starving, the house is in total disrepair. His experience with the tree has awakened in him some sense of the interconnectedness of all things and of his own obligation to the preservation of life. He commits himself to the unorthodox family he has inherited, fixes up the old house, and earns money to feed them.

One could perhaps have entitled this story, too, "The Tree of Knowledge," for when later the man discovers that the pine has been felled in a winter storm, it seems to symbolize the masculine patriarchal destructive knowledge so hated and feared by women local colorists. It is this knowledge that has died in the man in his assumption of the role of homemaker. But earlier, when the man had encountered the tree in its natural setting, the tree had yielded a knowledge of the sacredness of all things and of their interdependence. It is this matriarchal knowledge rooted in the world of nature—most fully expressed in the works of Sarah Orne Jewett—that Freeman believes must prevail. In the end, she urges, even men must learn it. For, as she concludes in this wise story: "Who shall determine the limit at which the intimate connection and reciprocal influence of all forms of visible creation upon one another may stop?" (79–80).

Notes

Notes: Introduction

1. M. E. W. S., "The 'Atlantic' Feast Day," n.d., newspaper clipping, Houghton MS Am 1743.1 (71), Houghton Library, Harvard University. This and following materials from the Houghton Library are published by permission of the Houghton Library, Harvard University.

2. The notable, although unpublished, exceptions are Susan Allen Toth, "More Than Local Color: A Reappraisal of Rose Terry Cooke, Mary Wilkins Freeman and Alice Brown" (Ph.D. diss., University of Minnesota, 1969), and Robert Lowell Russell, "The Background of the New England Local Color Movement" (Ph.D. diss., University of North Carolina, 1968). Ann Douglas Wood's "The Literature of Impoverishment: The Women Local Colorists in America 1865–1914," *Women's Studies* 1, no. 1 (1972): 3–46, presents, to my mind, an erroneous view of the local colorists. Also relevant are: Perry D. Westbrook, *Acres of Flint, Writers of Rural New England 1870–1900* (Washington, D.C.: Scarecrow, 1951; rev. ed., 1981), and Babette Levy, "Mutations in New England Local Color," *New England Quarterly* 19 (September 1946): 338–58.

3. See Radicalesbians, "The Woman Identified Woman," *Notes from the Third Year: Women's Liberation* (New York, 1971): 81–84.

4. Nancy K. Miller, *The Heroine's Text: Readings in the French and English Novel, 1722–1782* (New York: Columbia University Press, 1980), p. 4.

5. See Elizabeth Ammons, *Edith Wharton's Argument with America* (Athens: University of Georgia Press, 1980).

6. Nancy Sahli, "Smashing: Women's Relationships Before the Fall," *Chrysalis no. 8* (Summer 1979): 17–27.

✓7. Ellen Moers, *Literary Women* (Garden City, N.Y.: Anchor, 1977), p. 67.

8. I follow here the definition developed by Ulrich Weisstein in *Einführung in der Vergleichende Literaturwissenschaft* (Stuttgart: Kohlhammer, 1968), pp. 137–38. Other works which I found useful in formulating my ideas about the literary relationships among these women include: Ihab H. Hassan, "The Problem of Influence in Literary History: Notes Towards a Definition," *Journal of Aesthetics and Art Criticism* 16, no. 1 (September 1955): 66–76; Haskell M. Block, "The Concept of Influence in Comparative Literature," *Yearbook of Comparative and General Literature* 7 (1958): 30–37; Claudio Guillén, "The Aesthetics of Influence Studies in Comparative Literature," *Studies in Comparative Literature*, no. 23 (1959): 175–92; René Wellek, "Periods and Movements in Literary History," *English Institute Annual 1940* (New York: Columbia University Press, 1941): 73–93.

9. Perry D. Westbrook, *Mary Wilkins Freeman* (New York: Twayne, 1967), p. 115.

10. Elizabeth Stuart Phelps, *Chapters from a Life* (Boston: Houghton Mifflin, 1896), p. 151.

11. Frank Luther Mott, *A History of American Magazines,* vol. 2 (1850–65) (Cambridge: Harvard University Press, 1938), p. 501.

12. *Atlantic Monthly* 1, no. 7 (May 1858): 891.

13. Fred Lewis Pattee, *The Development of the American Short Story: An Historical Survey* (New York: Harper, 1923), p. 168.

14. Everett Carter, *Howells and the Age of Realism* (Hamden, Conn.: Archon, 1966), p. 118.

15. Helen McMahon, *Criticism of Fiction: A Study of Trends in the Atlantic Monthly 1857–1898* (New York: Twayne, 1952; reprint ed. 1973), p. 14.

16. Bernard R. Bowron, Jr., "Realism in America," *Comparative Literature* 3, no. 3 (Summer 1951): 268–85. Further references follow in the text. Other works on the local color movement that I found useful include: Alice Hall Petry, "Universal and Particular: The Local-Color Phenomenon Reconsidered," *American Literary Realism 1870–1910* 12, no. 1 (Spring 1979): 111–26; Robert D. Rhode, *Setting in the American Short Story of Local Color 1865–1900* (The Hague: Mouton, 1975); *The Local Colorists, American Short Stories 1857–1900,* ed. Claude M. Simpson (New York: Harper, 1960); Donald A. Dike, "Notes on Local Color and Its Relation to Realism," *College English* 14, no. 2 (November 1952): 81–88; Robert P. Falk, "The Rise of Realism 1871–91," *Transitions in American Literary History,* ed. Harry Hayden Clark (Durham: Duke University Press, 1954; reprint ed. 1967), pp. 381–442; and Benjamin T. Spencer, "Regionalism in American Literature," *Regionalism in America,* ed. Merrill Jensen (Madison: University of Wisconsin Press, 1951), pp. 219–60.

17. Bowron, pp. 275–76. See also Sydney E. Ahlstrom, *A Religious History of the American People* (New Haven: Yale University Press, 1972), pp. 418–27.

18. See Barbara Welter, "The Feminization of American Religion: 1800–1860," *Clio's Consciousness Raised,* ed. Mary Hartman and Lois W. Banner (New York: Harper, 1974), pp. 137–57, and for a more negative view of the phenomenon, Ann Douglas, *The Feminization of American Culture* (New York: Avon, 1977).

Notes: Chapter 1
Toward the Local Colorists: A Theoretical Sketch of Their Sources

1. Erich Auerbach, *Mimesis: The Representation of Reality in Western Literature,* tr. Willard Trask (Princeton: Princeton University Press, 1953; reprint ed. Garden City, N.Y.: Anchor, 1957), p. 308.

2. See Nancy K. Miller, "The Exquisite Cadavers: Women in Eighteenth-Century Fiction," *Diacritics* 5, no. 4 (Winter 1975): 37–43, as well as her *The Heroine's Text* (New York: Columbia University Press, 1980).

3. Ian Watt sees *Pamela* as a Cinderella plot, in *The Rise of the Novel: Studies in Defoe, Richardson and Fielding* (Berkeley: University of California Press, 1957), p. 204, and James R. Foster sees it as an example of the Griselda pattern, in *History of the Pre-Romantic Novel in England* (New York: Modern Language Association, 1949), p. 109.

4. Charlotte Lennox, *Henrietta*, 2 vols. in 1 (1758; reprint ed. New York: Garland, 1974), 1:12. Further references to this edition follow in the text.

5. Watt, p. 166.

6. Christine de Pisan, "L'Epistre au dieu d'amours," *Oeuvres Poétiques de Christine de Pisan*, in 3 vols. (Paris: Librairie de Firman Didot, 1885; reprint ed. 1965), 2:1–27. The passage cited is line 397. Further references follow in the text. My translation.

7. Jane Anger, "Her Protection for Women," *by a Woman writt: Literature from Six Centuries by and about Women*, ed. Joan Goulianos (Indianapolis: Bobbs-Merrill, 1973), pp. 23–29. See also Helen Andrews Kahin, "Jane Anger and John Lily," *Modern Language Quarterly* 8 (March 1947): 31–35.

8. Joyce M. Horner, *The English Women Novelists and Their Connection with the Feminist Movement* (1688–1797), *Smith College Studies in Modern Languages* 9, nos. 1–3 (October 1929; January and April 1930): 124.

9. Mary Delariviere Manley, *The Adventures of Rivella* (1714); reprint ed. in *The Novels of Mary Delariviere Manley*, ed. Patricia Köster, 2 vols. (Gainesville, Fla.: Scholars' Facsimiles and Reprints, 1971), 2:7–8. Further references to this edition follow in the text. Other critics who have noted the strain of "critical awareness" in Manley's work are Köster, Introduction to *The Novels of Mary Delariviere Manley*, 1:v–xxvii, and Delores Palomo, "A Woman Writer and the Scholars: A Review of Mary Manley's Reputation," *Women & Literature* 6, no. 1 (Spring 1978): 36–46.

10. Jane Barker, *A Patch-Work Screen for the Ladies* (London: E. Curll and T. Payne, 1723), p. 7. Further references to this edition follow in the text.

11. Sarah Fielding, *The Adventures of David Simple* (1744; reprint ed. New York: Dutton, 1904), p. 110. Further references to this edition follow in the text.

12. Eliza Haywood, *The History of Miss Betsy Thoughtless*, 4 vols. (London: T. Gardner, 1762), 1:129–30. Further references to this edition follow in the text.

13. Eliza Haywood, *Anti-Pamela*, (1741; reprint ed. Ann Arbor, Mich.: Xerox University Microfilms, 1976), pp. 2–3.

14. Charlotte Lennox, *The Female Quixote* (1752; reprint ed. London: Oxford University Press, 1970), p. 23. Further references to this edition follow in the text.

15. On Lennox's influence on Edgeworth, see Duncan Isles, "Johnson, Richardson, and *The Female Quixote*," in *The Female Quixote*, p. 425. On Edgeworth's American influence, see Nina Baym, *Woman's Fiction: A Guide to Novels by and about Women in America, 1820–1870* (Ithaca: Cornell Unviersity Press, 1978), p. 29.

16. On Child, see Baym, pp. 52–53; Margaret Fuller, *Woman in the Nineteenth Century* (Boston: Jewett, 1855), p. 130.

17. Sandra M. Gilbert and Susan Gubar, *The Madwoman in the Attic: The Woman Writer and the Nineteenth-Century Literary Imagination* (New Haven: Yale University Press, 1979), p. 149.

18. Maria Edgeworth, *Castle Rackrent* (1800) in *Tales and Novels*, 10 vols. (New York: Harper, 1835), 1:11. Further references to this edition follow in the text.

19. O. Elizabeth McWhorter Harden, *Maria Edgeworth's Art of Prose Fiction* (The Hague: Mouton, 1971), p. 114.

20. Of course the contrast between urban and rural is one of the oldest themes in literature. It also appears in novels of manners, such as Fanny Burney's *Evelina* and other sentimentalist works in which the country ingenue is exposed to the wiles and wickedness of the city; however, in Edgeworth the emphasis is different. The reality of the country is substantial; it provides a real counterweight to the city for perhaps the first time in modern fiction.

21. Maria Edgeworth, *The Absentee* (1812) in *The Novels of Maria Edgeworth*, 12 vols. (New York: Dodd, Mead, 1893), 6:2. Further references to this edition follow in the text.

22. Eliot was largely contemporary with the American local colorists and therefore cannot really be seen as an influence, though she sustained a personal friendship with Harriet Beecher Stowe (see chapter 3). Another possible tributary that contributed to the American local colorists came from the French provincial realists, especially George Sand, of whom Sarah Orne Jewett was particularly enamored. However, to trace the French connection would require another lengthy disquisition, so I choose in this study to remain within the largely self-contained Anglo-American tradition.

Notes: Chapter 2
Toward the Local Colorists: Early American Women's Traditions

1. Susanna Rowson, *Charlotte Temple* (1794; Brattleborough, Vt.: William

Fassenden, 1813), p. 154. Further references to this edition follow in the text.

2. Nina Baym, *Woman's Fiction: A Guide to Novels by and about Women in America 1820–1870* (Ithaca: Cornell University Press, 1978), p. 52.

3. Tabitha Tenney, *Female Quixotism*, 2 vols. (Boston: I. Thomas and E. T. Andrews, 1801), 1:6. Further references follow in the text.

4. Baym, p. 22.

5. Catharine Sedgwick, *A New-England Tale* (New York: E. Bliss and E. White, 1822), p. 118.

6. Nancy K. Miller identified a "euphoric" as well as a "dysphoric heroine's text," *The Heroine's Text* (New York: Columbia University Press, 1980), p. xi.

7. Hannah Lee, *Elinor Fulton* (Boston: Whipple and Damrell, 1837), p. 109.

8. Augusta J. Evans, *St. Elmo* (1866; New York: Carleton, 1867), p. 8. A further reference to this edition follows in the text.

9. Barbara Welter, "The Cult of True Womanhood: 1820–1860," *American Quarterly* 18, no. 2, pt. 1 (Summer 1966): 151–74.

10. Sarah Josepha Hale, *Northwood: A Tale of New England*, 2 vols. in 1 (Boston: Bowles & Dearborn, 1827), 1:4. Further references to this edition follow in the text.

11. Of course, Washington Irving's *The Sketch-Book* (1819–20) originated the genre; indeed was the earliest work that could properly be called short stories. And Mitford claims to have derived her "sketches" from Irving. However, his pieces remain essentially romantic; whereas Mitford's are really the first that are authentically realistic. The American women writers derived undoubtedly from Mitford rather than Irving.

12. Sarah Josepha Hale, *Sketches of American Character* (1829; Boston: Freeman Hunt, 1831), p. 12.

13. Catharine Sedgwick, *Tales and Sketches* (Philadelphia: Carey, Lea and Blanchard, 1835), pp. 151–52.

14. Charlotte A. Jerauld, *Chronicles and Sketches of Hazelhurst*, ed. Henry Bacon (Boston: A. Tompkins, 1850), p. 364. Further references to this edition follow in the text.

15. Emily Chubbuck, *Alderbrook* (1846; Boston: Ticknor & Co., 1847), p. 11.

16. On Stowe, see Edward Wagenknecht, *Harriet Beecher Stowe: The Known and the Unknown* (New York: Oxford University Press, 1965), p. 154. The Cooke letter is: ALS, Rose Terry to F. L. Olmstead, 15 January 1856, Rose Terry Cooke Collection (#6651-e), Clifton Waller Barrett Library, University of Virginia Library.

17. Mary Clavers [Caroline Kirkland], *A New Home—Who'll Follow? Or, Glimpses of Western Life* (1839; reprint ed. New York: Garrett, 1969), p. vi. Further references to this edition follow in the text.

18. Robert Lowell Russell, "The Background of the New England Local Color Movement" (Ph.D. diss., University of North Carolina, 1968), p. 31.

Notes: Chapter 3
Annie Adams Fields and Her Network of Influence

1. Martha Saxton, *Louisa May: A Modern Biography of Louisa May Alcott* (Boston: Houghton Mifflin, 1977), p. 195.

2. Tillie Olsen, "A Biographical Interpretation," *Life in the Iron Mills or the Korl Woman* (Old Westbury, N.Y.: Feminist Press, 1972), p. 90. Further references to this article follow in the text.

3. Forrest Wilson, *Crusader in Crinoline: The Life of Harriet Beecher Stowe* (Philadelphia: Lippincott, 1941), p. 451. Further references follow in the text.

4. As cited in James C. Austin, *Fields of the Atlantic Monthly: Letters to an Editor, 1861–70* (San Marino, Calif.: The Huntington Library, 1953), pp. 277–78.

5. As cited in Austin, p. 106.

6. *Chapters from a Life* (Boston: Houghton Mifflin, 1896), p. 108.

7. Mark A. DeWolfe Howe, *Memories of a Hostess* (Boston: Atlantic Monthly, 1922), p. 7.

8. Stowe to Eliot, 26 September 1872, as cited in Cortes W. Cavanaugh, "The Friendship Between George Eliot and Harriet Beecher Stowe" (type-script monograph, Houghton Library, Harvard University), p. 10.

9. As cited in Rosamond Thaxter, *Sandpiper: The Life and Letters of Celia Thaxter* (Sanbornville, N.H.: Wake-Brook House, 1962), p. 179.

10. For further information on this relationship, see Josephine Donovan, "The Unpublished Love Poems of Sarah Orne Jewett," *Frontiers* 4, no. 3 (Autumn 1979): 26–31, and Josephine Donovan, *Sarah Orne Jewett* (New York: Ungar, 1980).

11. William Dean Howells, "Recollections of an Atlantic Editorship," *Criticism and Fiction,* ed. Clara Marburg Kirk and Russell Kirk (New York: New York University Press, 1959), p. 193. See also Edd Winfield Parks, *Charles Egbert Craddock* (*Mary Noailles Murfree*) (Chapel Hill: University of North Carolina Press, 1941), pp. 122–23. A further reference to Parks follows in the text.

12. As cited in George McMichael, *Journey to Obscurity: The Life of Octave Thanet* (Lincoln: University of Nebraska Press, 1965), p. 176.

13. *The Letters of Sarah Orne Jewett,* ed. Annie Adams Fields (Boston: Houghton Mifflin, 1911), p. 248.

14. Willa Cather, "148 Charles Street," *Not Under Forty* (New York: Knopf, 1953), p. 67. A further reference follows in the text.

15. "Miss Jewett" is in *Not Under Forty,* pp. 76–95; the interview is in *Phila-*

delphia Record 9 August 1913, reprinted in *The Kingdom of Art: Willa Cather's First Principles and Critical Statements 1893–1896,* ed. Bernice Slote (Lincoln: University of Nebraska Press, 1966), pp. 446–49. See Donovan, *Sarah Orne Jewett,* chapter 6, for a further discussion of this interview and of the Jewett–Cather relationship.

16. ALS, Cather to Jewett, 18 November [1908], Houghton Library, Harvard University. In an earlier letter, 10 May [1908], Houghton Library, Cather speaks of keeping two Jewett stories, "A White Heron" and "The Dulham Ladies," with her always.

17. *Letters of Sarah Orne Jewett,* p. 249.

18. ALS, Cather to Jewett, 24 October [1908], Houghton Library, Harvard University.

19. The South Berwick visit is noted in R. W. B. Lewis, *Edith Wharton: A Biography* (New York: Harper, 1965), p. 150; the Charles Street visits in ALS, Wharton to Fields, n.d., Houghton bMS Am 2001(102), Houghton Library, Harvard University.

20. ALS, Fields to Jewett, n.d., Houghton bMS Am 1743.1(33)33, Houghton Library, Harvard University.

21. Edith Wharton, *A Backward Glance* (New York: Scribner's, 1933; reprint ed. 1962), p. 293.

22. ALS, Rose Terry Cooke to Fields, 28 September 1884, Houghton Library, Harvard University.

23. ALS, Jewett to Cooke, 28 September [1884], Manuscript Collections, The Connecticut Historical Society, Hartford, Connecticut. Published by permission of the Society.

24. ALS, Fields to Jewett, n.d., Houghton bMS Am 1743.1(33)95. See also ALS, Fields to Jewett, n.d., bMS Am 1743.1(33)5, Houghton Library, Harvard University.

25. Sarah Orne Jewett, *Deephaven and Other Stories,* ed. Richard Cary (New Haven: College and University Press, 1966), p. 32.

26. *Letters of Sarah Orne Jewett,* p. 47.

27. ALS, Jewett to Fields, n.d., Houghton bMS Am 1743.1(117)14, Houghton Library, Harvard University.

28. Harriet Prescott Spofford, "Rose Terry Cooke," Elizabeth Stuart Phelps et al., *Our Famous Women* (Hartford: Worthington & Co., 1884), p. 204. Significantly, Cooke wrote the chapter on Stowe in this collection.

29. Jay Martin, *Harvests of Change: American Literature 1865–1914* (Englewood Cliffs, N.J.: Prentice-Hall, 1967), p. 139.

30. Carol Farley Kessler, "'The Woman's Hour': Life and Novels of Elizabeth Stuart Phelps (1844–1911)" (Ph.D. diss., University of Pennsylvania, 1977), p. 110.

31. Kessler, p. 181.

32. Jewett, manuscript diary, 1869, entries for 2 September 1869 and 2 October 1869, Houghton Library, Harvard University.

33. ALS, Jewett [to Fields?], 4 December 1877, Houghton bMS Am 1743(255)1, Houghton Library, Harvard University.

34. ALS, Fields to Jewett, n.d., Houghton bMS Am 1743.1(33)87, Houghton Library, Harvard University.

35. ALS, Phelps to Jewett, n.d., Houghton bMS Am 1743(227), Houghton Library, Harvard University.

36. Kessler, p. 212.

37. ALS, Mary E. Wilkins to Jewett, 16 March [1899], Houghton Library, Harvard University.

38. ALS, Fields to Jewett, n.d., Houghton bMS Am 1743.1(33)88, and ALS, Wilkins to Fields, 29 November 1896, Houghton Library, Harvard University.

39. As cited in Edward Foster, *Mary E. Wilkins Freeman* (New York: Hendricks House, 1956), p. 88. The stories are actually "Three Deaths" and "A White Heron."

40. Perry D. Westbrook, *Mary Wilkins Freeman* (New York: Twayne, 1967), p. 52.

41. ALS, Wilkins to Mary Louise Booth, 12 February 1885, and ALS, Wilkins to Booth, 17 February 1885, Mary Eleanor Wilkins Freeman Collection (#7407), Clifton Waller Barrett Library, University of Virginia Library. Susan Allen Toth's "Sarah Orne Jewett and Friends: A Community of Interest," *Studies in Short Fiction* 9, no. 3 (Summer 1972): 233–41, was helpful to me in preparing this chapter.

Notes: Chapter 4
Harriet Beecher Stowe and the Emergence of a Female Arcadia

1. Edward Wagenknecht, *Harriet Beecher Stowe: The Known and the Unknown* (New York: Oxford University Press, 1965), p. 139.

2. As cited in Forrest Wilson, *Crusader in Crinoline: The Life of Harriet Beecher Stowe* (Philadelphia: Lippincott, 1939), p. 547. Further references will follow in the text.

3. As cited in Wagenknecht, p. 97.

4. A thesis convincingly argued by Margaret Wyman, "Harriet Beecher Stowe's Topical Novel on Woman Suffrage," *New England Quarterly* 25, no. 3 (September 1952): 389–91.

5. I acknowledge here my indebtedness to two Stowe bibliographies: Margaret Holbrook Hildreth, *Harriet Beecher Stowe: A Bibliography* (Hamden, Conn.: Archon, 1976), and Jean W. Ashton, *Harriet Beecher Stowe: A Reference Guide* (Boston: G. K. Hall, 1977). Portions of this chapter appear

in Josephine Donovan, "Harriet Beecher Stowe's Feminism," *American Transcendental Quarterly,* no. 48–49 (Summer, 1982).

6. Harriet Beecher Stowe, *Regional Sketches: New England and Florida,* ed. John R. Adams (New Haven: College and University Press, 1972), p. 31.

7. Stowe, "Cousin William," *The Mayflower; Or, Sketches of Scenes and Characters Among the Descendents of the Pilgrims* (New York: Harper, 1843), p. 149.

8. Barbara Berg, *The Remembered Gate: Origins of American Feminism, the Woman and the City 1800–1860* (New York: Oxford University Press, 1978).

9. Reprinted in *Regional Sketches,* pp. 62–74. References to this edition follow in the text.

10. See Jean Kennard, *Victims of Convention* (Hamden, Conn.: Archon, 1978), pp. 10–20, on this pervasive device.

11. From *Men of Our Times,* as cited in Wagenknecht, p. 180.

12. Wilson, pp. 453–54. Stowe also wrote about Truth in "Sojourner Truth, The Libyan Sibyl," *Atlantic Monthly* 11, no. 66 (April 1863): 473–81.

13. Stowe, *The Minister's Wooing* (1859; reprint ed. Ridgewood, N.J.: Gregg Press, 1968), p. 110. Further references to this edition follow in the text.

14. On a similarly feminized Christianity in *Uncle Tom's Cabin,* see Elizabeth Ammons, "Heroines in *Uncle Tom's Cabin,*" *American Literature* 49, no. 2 (May 1977): 161–79.

15. *Letters of Sarah Orne Jewett,* ed. Annie Adams Fields (Boston: Houghton Mifflin, 1911), p. 47. Jewett did recant this criticism, however, as noted earlier, chapter 3.

16. Wilson, p. 428.

17. As cited in James C. Austin, *Fields of the Atlantic Monthly: Letters to an Editor, 1861–70* (San Marino, Calif.: The Huntington Library, 1953), p. 291.

18. Austin, p. 292.

19. Stowe, *The Pearl of Orr's Island: A Story of the Coast of Maine* (1862; Boston: Houghton Mifflin, 1896), pp. 176–77. Further references to this edition follow in the text.

20. Katherine T. Jobes, "From Stowe's Eagle Island to Jewett's 'A White Heron,'" *Colby Library Quarterly* 10, no. 8 (December 1974): 515–21. Elizabeth Stuart Phelps has a similar scene in *The Story of Avis* (1877) in which Philip Ostrander refrains from killing a beautiful white bird.

21. Wilson, p. 532, details how Harriet came to write the *Fireside Stories,* citing a letter she wrote to Fields on March 2, 1869: "The origin is this: there was an amount of curious old Natick tradition that I could not work into 'Old Town Folks' without making the book too bulky."

22. Stowe, *Oldtown Folks* (1869; Boston: Houghton Mifflin, 1894), p. iii. Further references to this edition follow in the text.
23. Wilson, p. 80.

Notes: Chapter 5
Rose Terry Cooke: Impoverished Wives and Spirited Spinsters

1. Rose Terry [Cooke], "The West Shetucket Railroad," *Independent* 24:2 (12 September 1872). The Cooke bibliography prepared by Jean Downey has been invaluable to me for this chapter: "Rose Terry Cooke: A Bibliography," *Bulletin of Bibliography* 21, no. 7 (May–August 1955): 159–63, and *Bulletin of Bibliography* 21, no. 8 (September–December 1955): 191–92.
2. Seen in such stories as "Betsey Clark," *Putnam's* (August 1856); "Joe's Courtship," *Putnam's* (May 1857); "Rachel's Refusal," *Harper's* (November 1857); and, especially, "Home Again," *Huckleberries Gathered from New England Hills* (1891; reprint ed. New York: Garrett Press, 1969).
3. Other than *Huckleberries* (see note 2), Cooke's main collections were: *Somebody's Neighbors* (Boston: Osgood & Co., 1881); *The Sphinx's Children and Other People* (1886; reprint ed. New York: Garrett, 1969); and *Root-bound and Other Stories* (1885; reprint ed. Ridgewood, N.J.: Gregg Press, 1968). Further references to these editions follow in the text.
4. Mary Angela Bennett, *Elizabeth Stuart Phelps* (Philadelphia: University of Pennsylvania Press, 1939), p. 21, notes that the *Atlantic Monthly* Index lists this story as Phelps's; however, Phelps herself does not claim it as hers in her autobiography, *Chapters from a Life.* The story has all the features of a typical Cooke story: it begins *ab ovo;* it is set in Connecticut; the dialect is typical, as are the plot and characters.
5. Helen Papashvily, *All the Happy Endings* (New York: Harper, 1956), and *Nina Baym, Woman's Fiction: A Guide to Novels by and about Women in America 1820–1870* (Ithaca: Cornell University Press, 1978).

Notes: Chapter 6
Elizabeth Stuart Phelps: Burglars in Paradise

1. Lillian Federman, *Surpassing the Love of Men: Friendship and Romantic Love between Women From the Renaissance to the Present* (New York: Morrow, 1981), pp. 239–53, indicts the sexologists. Sahli's analysis is in "Smashing: Women's Relationships Before the Fall," *Chrysalis* no. 8 (Summer 1979): 17–27.
2. Carol Farley Kessler, "'The Woman's Hour': Life and Novels of Elizabeth Stuart Phelps (1844–1911)" (Ph.D. diss., University of Pennsylvania, 1977).

3. Kessler was the first to identify the *Gates* novels as Utopian works.
4. See Phelps, *Chapters from a Life* (Boston: Houghton Mifflin, 1896), pp. 140–41.
5. Phelps's main story collections were *Men, Women and Ghosts* (Boston: Fields & Osgood, 1869); *Sealed Orders* (Boston: Houghton, Osgood & Co., 1879); *Fourteen to One* (1891; Boston: Houghton Mifflin, 1897); *The Oath of Allegiance and Other Stories* (Boston: Houghton Mifflin, 1909); and *The Empty House and Other Stories* (Boston: Houghton Mifflin, 1910). Further references to these editions follow in the text. For this chapter the bibliography of Phelps's works prepared by Mary Angela Bennett, *Elizabeth Stuart Phelps* (Philadelphia: University of Pennsylvania Press, 1939), was invaluable.
6. Harriet Martineau's *A Manchester Strike* (1832) was perhaps the earliest of these. See P. J. Keating, *The Working Classes in Victorian Fiction* (London: Routledge & Kegan Paul, 1971).
7. Phelps, *Hedged In* (Boston: Fields, Osgood & Co., 1870), p. 2. Further references follow in the text.
8. Phelps, *An Old Maid's Paradise* (Boston: Houghton Mifflin, 1885), p. 85. Further references follow in the text.
9. Phelps, *Dr. Zay* (Boston: Houghton Mifflin, 1882), p. 88.
10. Phelps, *Burglars in Paradise* (Boston: Houghton Mifflin, 1886), p. 11. Further references follow in the text.
11. Phelps, *The Silent Partner* (Boston: Osgood & Co., 1871), p. 50. Further references follow in the text.
12. Phelps, *Beyond the Gates* (Boston: Houghton Mifflin, 1883), p. 141.
13. Phelps, *The Story of Avis* (1877; Boston: Houghton Mifflin, 1886), p. 122. Further references to this edition follow in the text.

Notes: Chapter 7
Sarah Orne Jewett and the World of the Mothers

1. See Josephine Donovan, "A Woman's Vision of Transcendence: A New Interpretation of the Works of Sarah Orne Jewett," *Massachusetts Review* 21, no. 2 (Summer 1980): 365–80, for an earlier version of this thesis. Some of the material in this chapter appeared in different form in Josephine Donovan, *Sarah Orne Jewett* (New York: Ungar, 1980).
2. *Sarah Orne Jewett Letters*, ed. Richard Cary (Waterville, Me.: Colby College Press, 1967), p. 52.
3. Jewett, Manuscript diary, 1871–79, Houghton Library, Harvard University.
4. *Letters of Sarah Orne Jewett*, ed. Annie Adams Fields (Boston: Houghton Mifflin, 1911), pp. 21–22. Further references follow in the text.
5. Jewett's main story collections are *Play Days* (Boston: Houghton, Os-

good & Co., 1878); *Old Friends and New* (Boston: Houghton, Osgood & Co., 1879); *Country By-Ways* (Boston: Houghton Mifflin, 1881); *The Mate of the Daylight, and Friends Ashore* (Boston: Houghton Mifflin, 1884); *A White Heron and Other Stories* (Boston: Houghton Mifflin, 1886); *The King of Folly Island and Other People* (Boston: Houghton Mifflin, 1888); *Strangers and Wayfarers* (Boston: Houghton Mifflin, 1890); *A Native of Winby and Other Tales* (Boston: Houghton Mifflin, 1893); *The Life of Nancy* (Boston: Houghton Mifflin, 1895); *The Queen's Twin and Other Stories* (Boston: Houghton Mifflin, 1899); and *The Uncollected Stories of Sarah Orne Jewett,* ed. Richard Cary (Waterville, Me.: Colby College Press, 1971). Further references to these follow in the text. Bibliographic tools which have proven most useful in the preparation of this chapter, as well as my other Jewett studies, include: Clara Carter Weber and Carl J. Weber, *A Bibliography of the Published Writings of Sarah Orne Jewett* (Waterville, Me.: Colby College Press, 1949), and Gwen L. and James Nagel, *Sarah Orne Jewett: A Reference Guide* (Boston: G. K. Hall, 1978).

6. Manuscript diary, 1871–79, entry for 13 July 1872, Houghton Library, Harvard University.

7. Phelps, *Chapters from a Life* (Boston: Houghton Mifflin, 1896), p. 9. See Howard Kerr, *Mediums and Spirit-Rappers and Roaring Radicals: Spiritualism in American Literature, 1850–1900* (Urbana: University of Illinois Press, 1972), for further details about this subject.

8. *Sarah Orne Jewett Letters,* ed. Cary, p. 91.

9. *Sarah Orne Jewett Letters,* ed. Cary, p. 21.

10. Jewett, *Deephaven and Other Stories,* ed. Richard Cary. (New Haven: College and University Press, 1966), p. 139. Further references to this edition follow in the text.

11. Pagination indicated in the text for this story and for "Miss Tempy's Watchers" (see below) is to this edition: *The Country of the Pointed Firs and Other Stories* (Garden City: Doubleday Anchor, 1956).

12. Annis Pratt, "Women and Nature in Modern Fiction," *Contemporary Literature* 13 (Autumn 1972): 476–90.

13. Louise Bernikow, *Among Women* (New York: Harmony, 1980), p. 30.

14. Nina Auerbach, *Communities of Women: An Idea in Fiction* (Cambridge: Harvard University Press, 1978), p. 10.

15. *The Country of the Pointed Firs* (Boston: Houghton Mifflin, 1896). Further references to this edition follow in the text.

Notes: Chapter 8
Mary E. Wilkins Freeman and the Tree of Knowledge

1. Mary E. Wilkins [Freeman], "The Tree of Knowledge," *The Love of Parson Lord and Other Stories* (1900; reprint ed. Freeport, N.Y.: Books for Libraries Press, 1969), p. 139. Freeman's main collections of stories include the following: *A Humble Romance and Other Stories* (1887; New York: Garrett Press, 1969); *A New England Nun and Other Stories* (New York: Harper, 1891); *Silence and Other Stories* (New York: Harper, 1898); *Understudies* (New York: Harper, 1901); *Six Trees* (New York: Harper, 1903); *The Givers* (New York: Harper, 1904); *The Fair Lavinia and Others* (New York: Harper, 1907); and *The Winning Lady and Others* (New York: Harper, 1909). Further references to these editions follow in the text. While Freeman continued to publish until the 1920s, I am limiting this study to that majority of her works published before 1910, on the theory that the New England local color tradition had run its course by then.

2. Cited by Edward Foster, *Mary E. Wilkins Freeman* (New York: Hendricks House, 1956), p. 143.

3. As cited in Foster, p. 95.

4. Freeman, *By the Light of the Soul* (New York: Harper, 1907), pp. 352–53. Further references follow in the text.

5. Freeman, *The Portion of Labor* (1901; reprint ed. Ridgewood, N.J.: Gregg Press, 1967), p. 244. Further references follow in the text.

6. See Donovan, *Sarah Orne Jewett* (New York: Ungar, 1980), pp. 60–64.

7. Wilkins [Freeman], *Pembroke* (New York: Harper, 1894), p. 187.

8. Freeman, *The Shoulders of Atlas* (New York: Harper, 1908), p. 78. Further references follow in the text.

9. Wilkins [Freeman], *The Long Arm, and Other Detective Stories* by George Ira Brett et al. (London: Chapman & Hall, 1895), pp. 60–61. See also Kathleen L. Maio, "'A Strange and Fierce Delight': The Early Days of Women's Mystery Fiction," *Chrysalis*, no. 10 (n.d.): 93–105.

10. As cited in Foster, p. 92.

11. As cited in Foster, p. 94.

Index